JUNGIAN REFLECTIONS ON SEPTEMBER 11

A GLOBAL NIGHTMARE

Jungian Reflections on September 11

A Global Nightmare

*Edited by Luigi Zoja
and Donald Williams*

DAIMON
VERLAG

The poem "Checkmate" is reproduced by permission of the poet, Lucio Mariani. It is to appear in *Echoes of Memory, Selected Poems of Lucio Mariani*, translated by Anthony Molino, to be published by Wesleyan University Press in 2003.

Cover illustration: The Tower of Babel
Pieter Bruegel (about 1525-69), 1563; Oil on oak panel, 114 x 155 cm;
Kunsthistorisches Museum Wien, Vienna
www.ibiblio.org/wm/paint/auth/bruegel/ (citation 1)
From the WebMuseum (master site: University of North Carolina, Chapel Hill) Copyright © 1994, 1995, 1996, 2002 Nicolas Pioch

ISBN 3-85630-619-6

Checkmate

I was born in Rockaway, below Brooklyn, on a strip
of land that looks like a fat finger stretching into the Atlantic.
I remember no woman who cherished my cradle or teenage
awe. And yet, it was special to grow up behind a hedge,
with the ocean every day in my eyes, special
to uncover the pride my father's Italian face couldn't hide
the time I brought my first accountant's paycheck home.
He wanted to play chess and, smoking but two cigarettes,
let me beat him unequivocally, on a combination rook-and-
                                                queen.
He ended by saying to always watch out for those treacherous
                                                towers
and the black-and-white crosses their long moves plot.
"Treacherous," he said, somberly: I remembered the word
with a smile that Tuesday, September 11,
as I raced to work through Manhattan.
And I recall his warning now
that I am dust scattered by an obscene blast
dust lost among the dusts of others undone
below a ravaged sidewalk, next to the leaf where
never will my father find me not even
to hold the hand I'd use to play him. I came from Rockaway
where I knew no woman's love or warmth:
may one now come and ask the white irises
to bloom in my name, faded, erased.

– *Lucio Mariani*

Contents

Preface

Throughout history, wars and other catastrophes have produced mass destruction far greater than what occurred on September 11, 2001 with the terrorist attacks in New York and Washington. Yet seldom has such a pervasive and all-encompassing shock been felt as with the brutal and unprecedented '911'. It seems we are all wounded and carry a symbolic imaginal scar. Has our world become a different place as a result? If so, in what ways? Along with the tragic aspects, what might this 'global nightmare' have to say to us? What is there for us to acknowledge and what old and new wounds have been opened? What sort of a legacy has been left behind?

These big questions and many more face us in the aftermath. In this book, the highly complex incident of 911 is circled and examined from many angles by a variety of writers who all share a training in depth psychology. What might a psychotherapist or depth psychologist perceive in such an eruption of shocking contents? Symptoms of such enormous force are not only frightening and painful: they also provide material to work with and, subsequently, meaning. Those familiar with the nature of the soul know that unexpected and painful developments potentially bring growth and change. That is, if we are ready, willing and able to accept, reflect and work with what we are given. It is hoped that this collection of essays will serve as a stimulus for other such efforts, individual and collective alike.

The events of September 11 were tragic, most of all for those directly involved, but the effects were felt worldwide. As devastatingly real as the attacks were, it might be worthwhile for us to also observe the developments as if they were a series of images from the unconscious, or a collective dream, and thus a potent source for information. Dreams, nightmares included, often provide messages of great importance to the dreamer. What do these images bring to us, our conscious selves? How do we receive and comprehend them, how do we bear them and what happens next? This was a 'nightmare' of gargantuan collective proportion and its in-the-face confrontative reality cannot be ignored: one and all, we are affected in inner and outer ways, and it has altered our experience and perception. Like a trauma in the life of an individual, this collective one is clearly a major reference point in our history.

In the interpretation of dreams, symptoms, images and emotions in the therapy room, it is generally not appropriate to 'rush in' and identify with one particular aspect, or to categorize. By providing the complexity of the whole with adequate space and allowing feelings to unfold, we enable the contents to reveal themselves and their meaning. Taking this sort of a therapeutic approach to 911 might also help towards finding a new attitude, increased consciousness and eventually a healing of the wounds.

When the first news reports went out, primary attention appropriately went to the victims. But then came speculation, accusations, justifications and a lot of fundamentalistic rhetoric: there were references to holy causes, matters of good and evil, and so forth. For many Americans, September 11, 2001 was felt as war on their previously safe and sovereign territory, a devastatingly cruel attack directly into the heart of their collective identity. What could ever have led to such a development? With the initial feelings of helplessness and vulnerability came the urge to 'do something' and there were calls for military action, invasions, crackdowns on foreigners and much more, all fed by the fear that further attacks, in whatever form, might well be on the way.

The world still looks in large part the same on this, 'the morning after': life moves on and the seasons unfold. But as with a nightmare, we are shaken by what was experienced in the dark night. What could the role of the analyst be here? Traditionally, most analysts have chosen to be very 'discreet', to comment little if at all with regard to political events, and to restrict their work to the analytic chamber. The magnitude of this event, however, has shaken many to speak out, to openly discuss a major collective issue for the first time, and to become active in other ways. They are contributing their attempts to understand what we have experienced, and are continuing to experience, as we strive to find meaning.

The idea for this collection of essays reflecting upon September 11 was born on that very day in 2001. Luigi Zoja, a recently transplanted Milanese analyst living in Katonah, New York, was struck hard by the events in his newfound city and home, and he began reflecting and writing: the fruits of this are to be found in the first essay of this book. He encouraged several Jungian colleagues to do the same and began to collect the results. A few months later, Don Williams of Boulder, Colorado joined him as co-editor. They felt an urgency to address the issue, to bring insight from their own fields of work and thought to this shattering event, and to search for deeper understanding.

We chose the Biblical Tower of Babel as our cover-motif. The hubris and vulnerability it has traditionally represented would seem appropriate to express the state of our world at the moment when September 11 occurred. Our lack of proportion, our inflation and our disharmony were parts of the setting and helped prepare the ground. While the cold-blooded attacks themselves cannot be justified, it is nevertheless our duty to acknowledge the imbalances in the world between North, South, East and West and in the state of the world's economy, the enormous gap between the haves and the have-nots: these are undeniable realities.

It is interesting and perhaps significant to recall that the IAAP (International Association for Analytical Psychology) held its triannual international congress just a few days before 911 in Cambridge, England and had chosen "2001" as its theme. Present time and global problems at the cusp of the Millennium were hot topics, with far more connections to sociocultural and sociopolitical dimensions than ever before at such a congress. Many participants from diverse parts of the earth took part in this forum for the first time. The state of the world today versus the timeless quality of the archetypal was a theme that flowed through numerous presentations. But there was and is a domination of Euro- and US-centricity in the membership of this organization and its writings, as in much of our environment, something to bear in mind as we ponder the context into which 911 erupted. We have our work cut out for us: a new equilibrium is needed and we must learn a new way of listening.

Here in 'safe Switzerland' where I happen to reside, we were affected by many 'after-shocks' in the days and weeks immediately following the events in New York and Washington: a horrible accident and fatal fire in one of the great Alpine tunnels; an amok shooting spree at a government meeting; the abrupt ending of the 'secure' national airline, Swissair; the crazed ramming of the cathedral doors at the abbey of Einsiedeln with his automobile by an angry young man; and more, all within less than a month. Colleagues in other parts of the world reported widespread similar phenomena.

Many of us and our families, friends and clients had forebodings, dreams of a great catastrophe approaching; people felt uneasy, there seemed to be a plethora of relationship crises, something was 'in the air'. Once the tragic event took place, how were we to understand it? What was our world coming to? Most of us were physically 'far from the scene' but we found ourselves caught in the midst of our own states of crisis. When it comes down to it, we are all in the same boat: we share one and the same planet. As was often heard in the days that followed, "Today we are all New Yorkers." The same could be said for other orientations, of course. There was a strong feeling of solidarity with whatever position one identified with. It has been anything but a time of apathy. The obvious difficulties notwithstanding, I am convinced it could also be a time of great opportunity for transformation, if only we avail ourselves of it. Our planet earth is a *corpus mundi,* a living organism formed and held together by the whole of its distinct parts. If any part is neglected, it affects the whole. The present is a crucial moment in time for respectfully acknowledging the differences and reevaluating old hierarchies with a critical attitude, as a means to arrive at a new and healthier balance. This is not merely a 'noble goal': it is a matter of survival.

Let us recall a piece of advice from Carl Gustav Jung, the Swiss psychiatrist who developed the ideas today known as Analytical or Jungian Psychology: he emphasized that changes in the greater world must begin within the individual. In becoming more aware, more conscious on an individual level, we are also contributing to an increased awareness in the world. The authors of these essays, by reflecting in their own ways on the implications and meanings of this moment in history and how it is affecting us, are hopefully stimulating others to move a little further in their own reflections. While different religious beliefs and generations and ethnic origins are represented, a common characteristic of each of the writers is that of being a Jungian Analyst, i.e., a psychotherapist trained in and practicing the psychology originated by Jung. With this mixture of individuals from different cultures and regions of the world, a diverse range of approaches to understanding is included. Nevertheless, it is obvious that Amero-European, Judaeo-Christian, male representation predominates here and it is hoped that individuals from other vantage points will be encouraged to make their own contributions.

A few years back, I had the good fortune of a close friendship with an older man who was increasingly concerned with the state of our existence on this planet. During the long final chapter of his life, he found ways to be both politically active and also a kind of troubadour of the soul. Though he had been a soldier in times of war, his fundamental position was to champion the role of 'the feminine' in our existence, that is to say, to cultivate attitudes traditionally associated with the feminine in each of us, such as our ability to listen, to feel and to assimilate: to allow 'the other', both in ourselves and in the outer world, to have its place and its voice. The absence of such an ability to include and to mediate between opposing forces is a one-sidedness, a monopoly, a rigidity that ultimately proves fatal. I believe my friend was correct in his observation and his concern, and that it would behoove us to take appropriate steps. The hour is late.

If we are not to destroy ourselves through inept relations with the planet and those with whom we share this home, we must honor and practice a more 'feminine functioning of the ego', so as to let the Tao, or Self, take its course. The individuals who, Jung says, can bear the tension of the opposites within themselves are those whose egos function in a more feminine way, countering the over-developed masculine ego and allowing the influence of the Tao, of yin-yang, to exist. Their egos allow things to happen in the psyche in contrast to the predominantly masculine-dominated ego of today's western world that rather tends to interfere: helping, correcting, negating, not leaving the simple growth of the psychic processes in place.[1]

---

[1] For a fascinating treatise on this subject, see "Commentary on 'The Secret of the Golden Flower'" in Jung, C.G., *Alchemical Studies*, CW13, Princeton, 1967

Throughout the developments since September, I have been reminded of the beautiful and true story of a rainmaker, related by the Sinologist and translator, Richard Wilhelm at the Psychological Club in Zürich in the 1920's. It was often retold by Jung in moments when there was a rigidity or blockage in a situation, or in someone's attitude. In brief, the story goes as follows:

There was a great drought in the land (China) which had taken on catastrophic proportions: the population and their animals were perishing. All known methods for a solution – religious, magical, superstitious – were applied, to no avail. Eventually the elders had no choice but to call upon the last resort, the 'rain-maker'. The fragile old man was summoned from a distant mountainous province. He requested only a small hut in a secluded valley, to which he retreated for the next three days. On the fourth day, clouds appeared in the sky, and then there was a heavy rainstorm, ending the drought. Wilhelm was so impressed and mystified that he sought out the old man and asked him how he had brought the rain. At first, the rainmaker denied any responsibility, but Wilhelm persisted, asking what had transpired in the previous three days. The rainmaker explained to him that he came from another country where the energies were in proportion, in balance with one another, quite different from the land of the drought. This whole area was out of Tao, he said: he had felt it immediately upon his arrival. Thus, he needed to retreat to his own space and regain his own Tao, or balance. Once that was accomplished, it was only natural that the rain began to fall on the land.[2]

---

[2] Heard in oral form from various friends of Jung: C.A. Meier, Aniela Jaffé and Liliane Frey-Rohn. For a written version, see Jung, C.G., *Mysterium Coniunctionis*, CW 14, Princeton, 1963, p. 419, fn 211

This anecdote recounted by Richard Wilhelm via Jung and others made a considerable impression upon me when I first heard it and I find it relevant in the present situation. Are we willing to approach today's global problems of imbalance in such a way? The rainmaker succeeded in bringing his own world into harmony and thereby influenced his surroundings, which then came into balance as well. Of course the outer circumstances today are far different, and we are living in a different time. The factors contributing to our present state of global imbalance are numerous and complex, interwoven with our histories and stories, much of it rife with conflict and pain. But, as in that province of China long ago, many of us are 'out of sync', or harmony, with ourselves and our surroundings, and our world is suffering terribly as a result. By working on ourselves, we may not be able to produce something as tangible as rainfall, but we can still make a contribution to the overall harmony of our surroundings and perhaps add a symbolic drop of rain at an opportune moment. The world needs every raindrop – in proportion.

The reasons for our exploitations and prejudices are manifold but they have a common root: our sense of balance has in many respects been lost. We have become so involved with 'doing' and with controlling things that our lives have in large part become devoid of meaning. What do we believe in today? It comes as no surprise that there is a lack of faith in today's world, a lack of trust. There is a long road to be traveled; a *conditio sine qua non* for the journey would be a common respect for the seemingly irreconcilable entities that all, in the end, belong to one and the same ephemeral force of life.

Robert Hinshaw
Publisher

September 11: Transatlantic Reflections

Luigi Zoja

> *Le XXIe siècle sera religieux ou ne sera pas.*
> The XXIst century will be religious, or will not be.
> André Malraux

> *(die Götter) haben sich selber einmal zu Tode
> gelacht! Das geschah, als das gottloseste Wort von
> einem Gotte selber ausging – das Wort "Es ist Ein
> Gotte."*
> (the Gods) one day killed themselves by laughing!
> It happened when the most godless utterance was
> spoken by a God – the utterance: "There is only one
> God."
> Friedrich Nietzsche

The author of this paper is a European analyst of Italian origin, now living in the U.S. In keeping with this change of landscape, I will break an atavistic rule of my background and will use the first person more freely to voice my thoughts and feelings. Acting under the urgency of the events of September 11, I will forego scholarly writing even though with my background it is the preferred, respectable style.[1] I will try to

[1] This article expands upon a talk, "Don't Widen the Atlantic," given at the Italian Cultural Institute of New York during a panel discussion on November 29, 2001. Thanks to Paolo Riani, the Director of the Italian Cultural Institute.

17

keep my reflections psychological yet I will not avoid at least touching upon other fields. I am writing under the impulse to foster a better understanding between Islam and the West.

To prepare the way for dialogue about Islam and the West, I first want to reflect on differences between the "West" and the "American West." Knowing both sides of the Atlantic, I feel that the unity of the "West" is often fictitious, hypocritical – a fragile mask. I have tried to tell my American colleagues things that Europeans often see but do not say in their professional or personal transatlantic conversations. Europeans are bound more tightly to old codes of politeness that prohibit criticism, especially direct criticism, of their interlocutor. Beyond cultural codes, however, Europeans are "older," more tired and skeptical, therefore prone to believe that energy poured into debates is often wasted. I believe, on the contrary, that the European attitude is a waste: one may criticize many things about Americans but not their willingness to listen, have a dialogue, and change if you prove to them that something is worth changing.

I. On "Divine Justice"

In the perception – conscious and unconscious – of many we entered an "Age of Hubris" when we made the passage from the 20th to the 21st century. In our "new age" human arrogance knows no limits. Tragically, our arrogance followed upon a century ruled by secular and rational values. In the perception of Nietzsche – later shared by Freud, Jung and all of us – our passage from the 19th to the 20th century witnessed "the death of God." In the 20th century Western culture became – at least officially – secular and rational. The tragedy of our combined arrogance and secular reason is that Man has replaced God as the supreme authority: From a psychological point of view, Man can feel as omnipotent as God.

Our modernity – or post-modernity – is characterized not by the absence of God but by the substitution of a "divinized" human for the divinity of God. We can observe, for example, the human usurpation of godlike power whenever biology and medicine manipulate or re-create life and attempt to abolish the limits imposed by time and age upon the body.

Though we may dispose of God as an abstract idea, declaring God dead, we cannot dismiss the practical function of a supreme limit or judge of our deeds.[2] The classical world knew a religious respect for limits. The gods punished those who wanted to be happy or powerful *without limit*, those who wanted to be like the gods. I have expanded upon this theme in an earlier work, *Growth and Guilt: Psychology and the Limits of Development*.[3] In this ancient model, hubris is inseparable from nemesis. It is characteristic of the stories of hubris and judgment that arrogance is punished by its own excesses rather than by an enemy. For example, in Herodotus (who invented historiography and whose model of explanation had unconsciously remained more myth than history) the Persian invasion of Greece is defeated above all by its unrestrained ambition (Books VI and VII): the fleet cannot find a large enough harbor and the army cannot maneuver because of its size.

As history gradually unleashed the pursuit of progress, growth, and omnipotence, the West abandoned all respect for limits. The limits, however, did not disappear. As happens with every mythology and religious principle, the archetypal respect for limits has been repressed and rendered uncon-

[2] Jung, C.G., *Nietzsche's Zarathustra. Notes on the Seminar Given in 1934-39*. Vol. I, Princeton University Press, Princeton NJ, 1988

[3] Zoja, L., *Growth and Guilt. Psychology and the Limits of Development*. Routledge, London & New York, 1995

scious but not abolished. Self-limiting factors still act upon us but without our participating consciousness.

Our limits surface again to consciousness in two forms. First, we re-encounter them in popular entertainment where hubris is punished. We flock, for instance, to the cinema to see stories of arrogant technologies that destroy their human makers, stories from *Frankenstein* to *The Terminator*, *The Titanic* to *Jurassic Park*. Secondly, science and common sense present us with the unwanted and often unexpected consequences of our technological advances. We know that our habits of excess spoil the environment, devour natural resources, raise the earth's temperature, change climate, extinguish plant and animal species, and replace forests with deserts.

Scientific forecasts echo the archaic tale of nemesis, the mythic punishment of hubris and greed. In the years between 1950 and 2000 humankind consumed more resources than in the whole of history till 1950 – this is greed. As population grows, consumption keeps increasing and the forecasts grow darker. The paralysis of transportation follows from the arrogant expectation that we should be able to travel anywhere anytime: In the year 2025, forecasts predict that U.S. citizens will waste 8000 centuries of their time sitting in stopped traffic. Most recently we saw the sudden ruinous devaluations of the stock market due to the intoxicating excesses and staggering failures of new internet companies.

Let us sum up: The myth of "Divine Justice" as punishment for excessive arrogance is more alive than ever in the psyche. Our unhesitating habits of excess produce consequences that point to our limits whether we wish to acknowledge those limits or not (archetypal expectation of justice). Divine justice, however unconsciously, holds the attention of both scholars and unsophisticated masses. The tale of divine justice screams out to be retold. Under these circumstances, the latent myth of punishment for limitless arrogance (nemesis punishing hubris) combines with a genuine need for Divine Justice. We long for a divine presence after the death of God (archetypal expectation of a divine element).

Our need for limits and for justice also has its risks. Such longing leaves individuals and groups vulnerable to possession by an avenger mythology. Groups will wish to believe that God will be revived by their avenging acts. When an avenging mythology seizes a group, the group's acts must possess the magnitude – the symbolic and the persuasive character – of divine acts if the group is to stay cohesive and to gather support. Here again is the danger: the unconscious identification with divine justice is as arrogant and dangerous as the illusion of omnipotence, the illusion of being "beyond good and evil."

Now let's move a step further. The most universally known modern myth of hubris-nemesis, of justice curbing limitless greed is Marxism. Although the myth was a constant presence in our collective consciousness for more than a century, practical Marxism failed. Communism is dead because it proved ineffective in a modern economy, even more so because Marxist prophecy went wrong. Communism was first and foremost a faith. As such, it could dismiss its economic figures but not its "religious" prophecy. Marx had foreseen for the industrialized world an increasing, tragic impoverishment of the masses, masses robbed by capitalists. But in the West the enormous increase of wealth, combined with social provisions, prevented the drastic opposition of classes anticipated by Marx. The success of the Western middle class created an acceptable situation rather than the conditions for revolution.

Yet, if communism as a state system has proved unviable, the same cannot be said of the *Marxist myth*. Marxist prophecy envisioned an increasing separation of the opposites (which analytical psychology has taught us to fear). The growing distance between the dispossessed and the rich would signify the victorious hubris of the powerful. Secondly, Marxist prophecy awaited the sudden reunion, the sudden reversal (revolution, enantiodromia) of the one-sided aggrandizement of the rich and the exploitation of workers. The reversal represented a return of natural balance – nemesis, justice!

The first stage of the Marxist myth – the triumph of greed – never saw the light in the Western nations. Although Marxist prophecy failed to materialize as expected, the prophecy *is* being realized today where Marx never anticipated it. It is precisely the dramatic increase of distance between the wealthy and the dispossessed that is now exploding – not between classes in a country but between "classes of countries" on a global scale.

When Karl Marx was still a baby (1820), the highest per-capita income of a country (at that time Great Britain) was approximately three times higher than that of one of the countries at the lowest end (India, China). In 1900, Great Britain was still at the top but its per-capita income had climbed to nine times that of the countries at the bottom of the list (Egypt and others). In the twentieth century statistics are incomparably more precise and also incomparably more tragic. The best average personal income (interestingly, not found in the U.S. but in Switzerland followed by Japan) ranks 500-600 times higher than the one of Mozambique (well over $40,000/year compared to less than $80/year). The first part of the Marxist prophecy is being realized but not as Marx had foreseen. The distance between "haves" and "have-nots" has grown dramatically but the tension is primarily between rich and poor countries, not classes.

The Mediterranean Sea, historically at the origin of Western prosperity, watches its nemesis. The dispossessed of the Middle East have nothing to lose beyond an idle life of hunger and illness. They try to escape their fate and risk suicidal trips on boats with scarcely enough fuel, boats so overcrowded that everyone must stand, and then they throw themselves at night against an European coast. At dawn, often the only task left for the Italian Coast Guard is to collect the human trash from the tourist beaches – anonymous corpses, victims of globalization.

The dispossessed come from countries where modernity may have penetrated but only in the form of objects, not of culture. The culture of the West has no place in these countries where the religious presence envelopes every aspect of life as it did in our Middle Ages. The religious domination of culture is particularly characteristic of people who consider their religion to be the radical legacy of Mohammed. Like Jews, with whom Muslims are archaically linked through shadow projections and with whom they remain aggressively tied, Muslims seeking refuge in Europe can survive without a physical country but not without a religious tradition. Similarly, when Jews lost their language or when they became secular, they never lost their religious culture.

In the founding myth of Islam there is nothing comparable to the statement of Christ that Caesar and God require separate obedience (in the episode in which Jesus shows Caesar's face on the coin (Matthew, 22:15-22; Luke 20:20-26). *The traditional Islamic coin has only God's face.* The profound difference between Islam and Christianity did not disturb the West as long as the West could sign good oil contracts and receive support in the Cold War against Communism.

Vast numbers of people have *not* gone through a cultural revolution (like the Renaissance or the Enlightenment, for example) leading towards modernity. For many such people belief in prophecy tends to be literal. Is it any wonder that the dispossessed are prone to accept prophets who promise them a restitution of enthusiasm, of meaning, and of dignity? Who

23

promise to transform a seemingly senseless life by gradually converting death into noble sacrifice and martyrdom? Among their followers the Al-Qaeda was able to transform meaningless suicides into something sacred (*sacri-fice*), into instruments of God. Why consume your life waiting for meaning, if meaning can *explode instantly* – together with your life?

Let us not be misled by the fact that some terrorists apparently spent their last years as peaceful bourgeois in the southern U.S. or in the north of Germany. If we want to look at the issue psychologically, we should – as in analysis – turn our attention to much earlier stages in the lives of the terrorists. What myth of "rebirth through sacrifice" nourished their souls while milk nourished their bodies? As we have seen on videotape, children 8 years old and younger have already been training for suicide attacks. The indoctrination of sacred death for future terrorists must therefore have started even earlier than 8 years of age. Do we envisage a military or a cultural and psychological response to teachers and to children educated in terror? If the first answer prevails, then we – we, the civilized West – may need to be ready to kill many children before they become adults.

Let's take another step. For reasons which are very complex (they pertain at once to culture, history, economics, religion, and so on) large masses of people, and sometimes entire countries, see the U.S. as the emblem of planetary hubris. They attribute to America the responsibility for the hubris of the whole modern world. The U.S. is seen as intentionally corrupting non-Western cultures – new markets! – by its greedy, materialistic example. Once characterized as the "Great Satan," the U.S. is a convenient carrier for persecutory, "totalitarian" projections of the shadow on a global – total – scale.

The U.S. is seen as persistently and inherently trying to enjoy its better standard of life – its "American way of life" –

at the expense of the lives of others. We must acknowledge, however, that the expression, "American way of life," has become outdated, no matter how "American" this way of life once was. In the 21st century the way of life is determined on a global scale by the global economy. The shares of its enjoyment are then unevenly divided between prospering countries (most visibly the U.S.) and the "victim" countries. This perspective corresponds to the Marxist view of "class struggle" when transferred to international relations where we may see, for instance, hemispheric struggles.

The founding fathers of America included the right to the "pursuit of happiness" in their 1776 Declaration of Independence. The American declaration fought for a new, humanistic morality. Today, this precocious proclamation may be perceived by America's enemies as a genetic disposition towards hedonism at the cost of spiritual values. To many the "pursuit of happiness" appears as the archetypal statement of American excess – hubris – rather than as an affirmation of human dignity and individual liberty.

It is enough to look at statistics to understand why the U.S. can symbolize hubris: With less than 5% of the world's population, the U.S. consumes more than 30% of the world's resources. It is not so obvious, however, why the U.S. should bear the whole responsibility for the "revolution of enjoyment" that we have watched in the West (American and European).

Modern, economically successful countries have passed through revolutions that modernized the value system. Recall, for instance, that the American Revolution of 1776 was preceded by the Industrial Revolution in England which had followed the path of the French Enlightenment which was preceded in turn by the Italian Renaissance. The Italian Renaissance, by the way, owed not little to the Arab blossoming of the Middle Ages, thus closing an interesting historical

25

circle. The U.S. is not alone in its consumer habits nor in its revolutionary consumer culture. Nowadays, Europe and Latin America, for example, also seem to be inspired by the same hubris as the U.S., and they immediately join the "American way of life" as soon as they can afford it.

We should, therefore, try to understand psychologically why hubris is seen as concentrated in the U.S. when it is shared by most global economies. A familiar and easily stereotyped enemy is the best enemy, and the U.S. satisfies all the requirements with its obvious dominance. For example, the U.S. has maintained an astonishing military superiority without interruption since the mid-1800s. In order to demonize American military power, critics and enemies tend ignore that never in human history has such an overwhelming military superiority been used with such restraint. It is true that in 1846-48, the U.S. took over half of what was then Mexico – a region almost as large as Western Europe – and occupied its capital. However, the seizure of Mexican territory was the main exception in U.S. military history. Not only has human history never witnessed such military superiority but history has never seen military superiority used with such restraint. Nonetheless, the psychological scar remains part of Mexican identity, and the rest of Latin America suffers a secondary trauma since it looked to Mexico for cultural leadership. In the course of the last 150 years, the Latin American fear of being conquered by North American greed has simply been transformed from a military into an economic fear.

Antagonism toward the U.S. often stems more from a cultural and psychological opposition than from hostile economic or military intentions. For example, although Italy and the U.S. shared no border and not much economic activity, anti-Americanism was one of the pillars of Fascist propaganda in the 1920s and 30s. It has been argued that there is an unbroken genetic thread which made anti-Americanism *reus-*

able by Italian Marxism after World War II.[4] But it is of course to the end of the Cold War and to the fall of Soviet Communism that we must look in order to understand the explosion of anti-Americanism on a planetary scale. Psychologically speaking, one of the collective polarities of the tense but effective balance which governed the world – capitalism versus communism – ceased to exist a decade ago. The collective psyche had to recreate a balance in the unconscious following the collapse of communism. Islam and the Roman Catholic Church are the two largest religions on Earth, each comprising more than one billion believers. Until the fall of communism, Islam avoided excessive criticism of the U.S. They were implicitly united with the U.S. by a common fight against communism. But, starting with the 1990s, Islamic leaders have explicitly blamed the "American way of life" for the excess of materialism and the lack of spirituality characteristic of our modern times.

Of course, we should not limit ourselves to a psychological perspective nor to interpreting unconscious processes. The leaders of poor and/or unstable Muslim countries who are affected by multiple internal problems, by doubtful democratic functioning, and by shaky public support, may find it politically very tempting to resort to anti-Americanism. The "capitalist plot" brandished by Communism focused only on the economic and not the cultural misery of the masses. The message of a great religion includes a criticism to capitalist inequality but goes far deeper than that. Third World masses, often economically poor since time immemorial, may not necessarily feel that the U.S. is responsible for their poverty. However, it is quite sure that if a teenager starts wearing jeans, eating at McDonald's, drinking beer, being sexually promiscuous, and/or acting ashamed of his Arab identity, his parents will resent the U.S. as merciless murderers of their

[4] Nacci, M., *L'antiamericanismo in Italia*, Boringhieri, Torino, 1989

culture: no Western soldier has killed their children, yet Hollywood has gradually been killing their exemplar models, their parents, and their ancestors. Parents have "good reasons" to resist the usurpation of their authority. In the genealogical tree, you can substitute a new generation but not an old one; you can replace the branches, not the roots. Indeed, elders know they are economically, not culturally poor. They may obscurely know that economical wealth can be achieved or reconstructed in short time: think of South Korea or think of West Germany after the Second World War. But a cultural identity, when gone, is gone forever: think of native populations in Australia, the Americas, Africa, and other continents.

The equation of the U.S. with Satan, put forward by several Islamic leaders, can explain both the economic and the cultural humiliation their populations have experienced. The triumph of hubris and greed is seen in globalization; and globalization is seen as an economic *and* a cultural Americanization of the world. Whoever is against globalization practices a certain amount of anti-Americanism.

The trend to oppose economic expansion is in no way limited to the uncultivated masses. In the West opposition is published in the well-educated milieus, including those in the U.S. as well. Only two months before New York's "Black Tuesday," the prestigious *Le Monde Diplomatique* published an issue which described American politics of the last decade – the last of the twentieth century and the first without the Communist adversary – as the test case for a "Second American Century" in the minds of some leading American politicians.

The tide of opposition to globalization grows as political leaders use the un-psychological attitude of the American administration to further manipulate envious populations. The "American administration"? Even my un-European ear perceives that this is offensive for the inhabitants of the rest of the "American" continent. From the Rio Grande to the Tierra del Fuego the grumble is the same: "'Americans' have even taken the name of the continent for themselves. It's a good symbol of their greed and of their attitude toward the rest of the continent." Sometimes this "grumble" gets clearly asserted in writing: You will find the criticism in the pages of well-known authors such as E. Galeano. Even European eyes may be surprised at the appropriation of the name, "American," and may revert to the writings of the founding fathers to find the "archetypes" of this country that is so difficult to define. The official voices of independence from Great Britain spoke of the "United States of America." When and how, therefore, did the shift, the "continental slip," occur? How is it possible now for the U.S. to act as though there were only one "America.," particularly when every official word has to be carefully filtered by the code of political correctness? In order to face the hostility of other countries, the U.S. government pours oceans of dollars into "intelligence." Why doesn't the U.S. organize a congress, a simple round table on this issue, an issue which doesn't require "intelligence" to be faced but simply common sense?

II. On September 11

On September 11, *more than* four commercial airplanes were hijacked: On September 11, our whole collective imagination was kidnaped, abducted, ripped from its usual soil and violently thrown back into a non-historical, archaic dimension. The whole calendar was stolen from us. We believed we had entered the third Millennium of the Christian era but we found ourselves in the direct grip of "arche-types" and "arche-times." We believed we were living in a logical and lay humanistic age. We found out, however, that we were experiencing myth. That is, not only was myth imposed upon us from outside; we also found ourselves thinking again mythically although we had not consciously chosen this kind of thinking.

Not even Hitler or Stalin had managed such an effect. They had not even dreamed of anything like this. Hot and cold wars had been tragic and mortal: an immense waste of human creativity transformed into deadly competition and destructiveness. Yet, the times had remained our still-recognizable modern times. Although Hitler and Stalin behaved at times as prophets, for the Western world they essentially remained enemy politicians.

Osama bin Laden speaks always and only in the name of (his idea of) divine justice. Two American preachers, Pat Robertson and Jerry Falwell, each capable of mobilizing vast audiences, equally declare that they see a similar hand of justice in what has happened. Fundamentalists of all persuasions know that they win a partial victory if they are able to bring the debate to a theological ground. American public opinion immediately rejects such an idea. We experience a fundamentalist triumph as rape.

Dreams echoing catastrophes similar to the one of the Twin Towers have become regular occurrences even for people who seldom had nightmares. Also common are dreams that attribute a degree of destructive omnipotence to Osama bin Laden. These dreams multiply among very different patients. The Associated Press has publicized a photo of the smoke surrounding the Twin Towers after the attack. Many consumers of this public image *see the profile of Osama bin Laden in the shape of the smoke*. Like saints, devils, Madonnas, and prophets in previous centuries and in remote places, a devastating divinity has appeared in the third Millennium and in the most modern of all skies – the skyline of Manhattan.

The same prophet of destruction has appeared on our domestic altar – the TV set, the center of our daily rituals. Osama bin Laden's voice, claiming to speak on direct behalf of the Almighty, has declared that Americans and their supporters will not live one more day in serenity. As every divine voice, it was aimed directly at our unconscious, attempting to skip the mediation of our rationality, of our conscious mind. To a noticeable extent, it has succeeded. In spite of daily and documented reassurances, many Americans, many Europeans, many citizens of the third Millennium found themselves victims of a psychological attack more undefinable and far-reaching than the physical one. The voice prophesied daily insecurity. The voice has kept its prophecy.

As we tend to pay attention mostly to outer reality, we claim to have discovered that terrorism, like everything else, has become global. The real discovery, on the contrary, seems to be the fact that decisive nightmares and paranoid fantasies, not terrorist acts, have become global. If I am correct in this analysis, we have regressed to a dangerously collective state. Part of our daily psychic functioning is being moved in dangerously direct ways by the deepest and most archetypal layers of our unconscious.

Delusional fantasies born in our inner world are recognizable as symbolic statements but suddenly these fantasies match an outside "delusional" reality. As a consequence we do not trust our psychic functioning or we do not trust our perception of reality – which comes to the same thing.

Through personal and historical self-criticism, we had come to accept that racism was the projection of inner persecutory fantasies. All of a sudden our persecutory fantasies are loose "out there." If we are normally responsive to the world, our mind gets contaminated by phantoms, and for the first time we might have an intuition of what psychotics regularly experience. A tragic political consequence of such contamination is that objective reality "allows" the reappearance of a form of anti-Semitism – anti-Arabism – on a global scale. Another highly visible consequence is the insurmountable difficulty faced by the U.S. administration when trying to reassure its citizens. At first everybody is advised to be on high alert as death might come from the sky or from the earth, at the mall or in the mail, in one day or one year, from undetermined sources. Following the anxious "alert" and often in the same message, people are exhorted to remain calm, to go about life as usual. Understandably, the oxymoron lends itself well to political cartoons (*New Yorker*, Nov. 26, 2001, p. 124). Psychiatrists, however, may wonder if they haven't seen this phenomenon described in their handbooks. Contradictory messages and allusive/persecutory patterns of expression, once the landmark of psychopathology, reappear unexpectedly as the most adequate way of describing reality.

If Jung was right in stating that the experiences of God and of the unconscious are not easy to distinguish from one another, then our dialogue with the unconscious is a genuine, non-formalistic kind of religious experience. Religion is not only an individual defense against insecurity by divinizing (idealizing) infantile memories of our parents, but also an archaic and historical fight with our inner world. Therefore, we must attempt to respect religious experience and at the same time to separate what is good from what is terrible. If, in sum, Jung's phylogenetic reconstruction satisfies us more than Freud's ontogenetic one, then we must recognize that a vast part of Western society has involuntarily fallen back into a primordial "religious" state. Our emotional state is "religious" in that it links (Latin: *ligare*) us again with the archetypal drives and images – both good and evil – out of which every historical religion has stemmed.

It has been observed – by Jung himself among others – that Christianity has curbed its Jewish origin in a more and more positive direction over time. Through its desperate fight against evil, the Jewish heresy bearing the name of Christianity has come to represent an extreme, one-sided kind of monotheism where the terrible face of God – which populated the Old Testament – almost disappears for the sake of goodness.

In this sense, the revival of Jewish religiosity after the *shoah* should not be seen only as an attempt to recover a national identity; it is also an attempt to recover a psychic balance. Traditional Jewish faith keeps one in touch with the terrible face of God, that is, psychologically acquainted with – and ready for – the *tremendum*. By losing faith in the existence of the *tremendum* one is unprepared to defend oneself from evils such as the Nazi "final solution" – actually, unprepared to believe that it might exist.

In the same sense, the excessively "positive" bent of Christianity was bound to ebb into the positivistic philosophy and ideology prevailing in the West and particularly in the U.S. (the "West of the West"). Science and technology are the logical modernization and realization of the "only good" ideology of the Christian world. Indeed, Christians believe in creation and pretend not to be interested in destruction. They claim to be concerned with good and not with evil. In its Eastern version (Marxism), the positivistic ideology attempted to transform politics into the science of the "society which abolishes evil." It failed. The Marxist failure only reinforced the one-sided optimism of its Western version. American "capitalistic society" expressed even more vigorously its faith in limitless economical and technological progress. And for a good decade the facts seemed to confirm that this faith was right.

I have expressed elsewhere the idea that a "right hand" of this society – Hollywood – has unconsciously provided a world of modern images and myths where tragedy has been banned.[5] Hollywood – films, film stars, television, etc. – has helped to shape unnatural heroes who are free of ambivalence and who therefore offer superficial tranquillity to the masses. What is worth noticing here is that, through this long education to optimism, the U.S. and the West as a whole have been particularly ill-prepared and fragile in front of the experience of pure destructiveness. Unable to conceive any more the wrath of God, we lack a trained imagination for archetypal evil – and this is probably why, following the recent events, many official voices in the West can speak of evil with a striking absence of psychological insight.

As analysts we of course wonder about our psychological relationship to evil. We fought to exhaustion to defend our patients from nightmares and paranoid fantasies. All of a sudden the work has regressed, and so we may ask: Could it be that our voice was untrue while the voice of nightmare and paranoia was true? Have we listened enough to them? Shouldn't we have taken paranoid fantasies more literally?

It is therefore worth noticing that we are watching a gigantic "return of the repressed" in the whole West. Of course, when we speak of a sudden archaic "religious experience," we speak neither of a conscious phenomenon nor of an institutional religion. People might describe their psychic states as superstitious experiences which they sarcastically try to devalue or as anxiety states, describing them with DSM terminology. But are these adequate explanations or reductive defense mechanisms, and if they are defenses, doesn't our behavior become part of the suffering itself?

Our society practically has not had the experience of the dark side of God for generations and centuries. When we were forced to see it – i.e., in Nazism (and Stalinism) – we tried not to recognize mass murder as something in itself but rather

---

[5] "Analysis and Tragedy" in Casement, A. (ed.) *Post-Jungians Today*, Routledge, London and NY, 1998

tried to sanitize it by relegating it to a chapter in pathology. On September 11, however, we suddenly saw "an angry god," a god of destruction, descending on Earth at the heart of the U.S. in the most unexpected place and moment.

The authors of the attack on New York and Washington had probably suffered deprivations unknown to the West – but not this one. The terrorists obviously had an imagination for mass murder. They had an ideological, a religious, and a psychological advantage: they were more familiar with the shadow side of existence.

The absolute "wrath of God" revealed in those who pretended to express it the existence of a modern fundamentalist heresy. Without entering the dispute of whether or not they belong to Islam, the attackers and their instigators can be described as ministers of a new, radical – and radically new – form of monotheism, which we could call "actualism."

Contradicting the connected principles of prophecy and redemption – which in various forms unite the three historical monotheisms (and even Marxism with its "redemption of the masses") – the "actualists" cannot wait for the organic fulfilment of prophecy in time. The epiphany of divine justice must take place in actuality in the double sense of an active and present reality. And the minister's task is to be the hand of God, to *act* in order to immediately bring about *his* will. The infinite – and indefinite – time horizon of metaphysical divine justice is rejected. The retaliatory wrath of God must be seen here and now. Yet, like many Jewish or Christian apocalyptic sects, when they announce the return of God, they are announcing the return of God in its darkest form.

We can't help noticing a striking contradiction. The "actualists" claim to be fighting for the restoration of a pure and traditional Islam. Yet, they express a radically modernistic, even consumer bias. Who has invented greedy impatience, the need to immediately reach your target, the implicit mistrust in metaphysics, distrust in a reward which will come in another dimension and another time? The answer is: modern consumerism. What we have called an actualist heresy of Islam seems to be driven by an impulse strikingly similar to the one dominating the hated "Great Satan." As we know from Jung's analysis, by concentrating oneself too much on a mortal adversary, on one's shadow, one becomes unconsciously infected by the shadow. No doubt, American – and Western – society is obsessed by the need to produce quick and visible results. But is Islamic fundamentalism still a metaphysical vision or has it been irrevocably transformed into a teaching for attaining practical and quick victories through destructive means?

As psychologists, it is our task not to limit ourselves to the outer events in spite of their magnitude. Can we, from an interior point of view, say that there is not only grief and loss but that our psyche has also gained a new vision, albeit tragically? Let us go back to a traditional tenet of analytical psychology: Opposite polarities should be held together as much as possible. Only through their *syn-thesis* (putting together both poles) can the symbol originate that will overcome a deadlock. The symbol is more than the simple sum of poles 1 and 2 – the symbol contains new, original elements.

Repression of an archetypal polarity causes a pathological imbalance, not only in the individual but in the whole of a society. In the Western history of the archetypal masculine-feminine duality, repression of the feminine has been held responsible for excessively rational or aggressive masculine attitudes. In the history of monotheism, repression of the terrible face of God in the passage from Judaism to Christianity has risked naive or hypocritical pretensions that one can be "only good." In the history of Euro-American modernity, the appearance of a positivistic faith, the belief that every increase in progress will imply an increase of happiness has brought many to believe that science will forever substitute magic, myth and other "superstitions." Science can even replace – and why not – religion because through technology human-kind proves more "creative" than any present Creator. Isn't this another way of describing the old problem of hubris? Isn't it equivalent to saying that hubris rampages, that our aware-ness of its natural polarity – nemesis – has been repressed? And, couldn't we agree that – at first sight, since history and society are much more complex than these simplifications – modern hubris is concentrated in the West? And, within the West, concentrated in the U.S.?

Haven't we been recalling the fact that – traditionally, archetypally – the most convincing, "divine" punishment of hubris comes from the instruments of arrogance which turn against its author?

> *Die ich rief, die Geister,*
> *Werd' ich nun nicht los*

screams Goethe's Apprentice Sorcerer. And we translate his scream: "I cannot control the powers I have activated."

In all these senses it was very easy to single out the U.S. and the Twin Towers in New York as an archetypal target. In the Holy Scriptures, as the Italian essayist A. Torno has recalled, the very expression *altissimus* (very high, in Latin) is reserved only to God. Exactly the same condemnation of too much growth toward the sky was expressed by Herodotus in the fifth century B.C. about the whole of Greek thinking (VII, 10). After God's death, however, the skies are empty, and their space is available for human colonization by skyscrapers and space stations. We would like to forget the warning given by the myth of Babel's tower to the three monotheisms since times immemorial. Once again: a vocation to colonize the skies is particularly present in American technology which invented aviation and New York's vaulting architecture.

The West and especially the U.S. embody the scientific and financial power of modernity, the cult of rationality, and the devaluation of the primitive and pre-rational part of our humanity. A typical example of one-sidedness and of the split of the opposites seemed concentrated in the U.S. but it was invisible to our Western eyes for the same reason a fish will not know it is wet. Pre-modern eyes are required to see our over-estimation of growth and progress. Pre-optimistic souls, imbued with the dark side of God, are required to ruthlessly conceive of the destruction of modernity.

We look at the September 11 tragedy now and wonder how we could have been so blind. Now, everything is so easy to "see." And it is easy to see how easy it was to conceive destruction and to perform it. We in the West really lacked a destructive and tragic imagination even though we were submerged by "apocalyptic" movies. We couldn't imagine the viciousness it took to sit in the most modern of the instruments of transportation – in first or business class to be even more vengeful – and turn it against the "Great Satan" who had developed the airline industry. The terrorists seemed to show that the most pre-modern man – he could have been a Neanderthal with a flint blade – can sit in the same cockpit with the most technologically advanced pilot and bend him to his will. The terrorists, however, performed their own act of hubris when they boarded in a U.S. airport to show that there is no safety within U.S. borders. Terrorism is variant form of hubris which calls for yet another nemesis – they try to exploit the self-punishing archetypal pattern of hubris. Actualism is a variant form of hubris; we can expect to see the terrorists summon their own nemesis.

It was easy for Islamic terrorists to claim that globalization is intrinsically evil, that globalization is the equivalent of Americanization, that American global power is hubris, and finally to exact divine justice by turning American power against itself. The global U.S. media power immediately brought to the whole world the image of nemesis in the ruin and death of September 11. The globalism and power of American media transmitted the images that its enemies were waiting to enjoy; it's in the nature of nemesis that hubris is turned against itself.

American success has been turned against itself in still other devastating ways. The American economy has spread throughout the world the principles of a free market and of privatization. We can imagine that American success has unconsciously inspired a rich Arab with the idea of building his own army and privatizing war and destruction – as noted by the German editorialist, Theo Sommer (*Die Zeit*, Oct. 11, 2001). Global nightmares are as vast as the globe. We fear that the head of this multi-national provider of death might have already started to privatize genocide. Should we consider our fear a persecutory fantasy or a realistic public threat?

The philosopher H. M. Enzenberger has noted that in an era of globalization even sacrifice becomes global. Here, we as Western psychologists must go further and once again acknowledge how naive we have been. The media kept speaking superficially of possible "suicide attacks" on the part of the fundamentalists. This description is limited by a Western, lay, and individualistic point of view that uses the word, "suicide," to define any person killing himself or herself. The phrase, "suicide attack," seems to fit only if we are predominantly interested in ourselves and the material aspects of our lives. I suspect that this reductive approach has again limited our imagination for destructive possibilities and thus limited our prevention of such attacks. None of the attackers, it seems, corresponds to the Western psychopathological definition of the suicidal personality. On the contrary, a fanatical religiosity and a devaluation of physical life – theirs and other's – created a longing for sacrifice, not to destroy life but to transform it into something believed to be sacred. It would be more adequate to speak of martyrdom (in Greek meaning "testimony") chosen by the terrorists and ironically publicized by the media of their enemies.

The World Trade Center Towers themselves – if we imagine a sarcastic terrorist – collapsed under their own weight, killing people tragically because of economic and cultural hubris, an arrogant claim to new heights of ambition. Suddenly and violently, the opposites were united again in the most unexpected way. The towers defying the sky collapsed to "ground zero." Only a thin front stands still, like a mask without the actor, a reminder of how the might of modern technology can be a frail facade. In frightening continuity, an upper and a lower city – one above and one under 14th Street, one belonging to the sky and one to the ground – were united. One world belongs to the man of technology; the other – stripped of electric power, water, and telephone connections – belongs to the Neanderthal man with the stone ax – or the box cutter, it doesn't matter – who was inspired by a leader significantly videotaped on the threshold of a rock cave. We have the image of modern man deodorized and dressed by Armani, the other covered with dust and smelling of burning human flesh. Five Star Hotels and Auschwitz hand in hand.

Not only are the opposites – the technological and the pre-technological – united in one morning but the two cultures are suddenly united in the global village. Television peers uninterruptedly into private aspects of life in the U.S. and simultaneously in Afghanistan, one of the poorest countries on earth, where the prophet of pre-technological man has fixed his stone-age residence. Almost overnight the weather page of the *New York Times* enlarged its geographical sketch to include a land outside U.S. borders. But it has not included Canada: the *Times* illustrates in color the weather of the U.S. and Afghanistan – side by side as if Afghanistan were not a Canada but a dark brother suddenly regurgitated by the unconscious, an unexpected contiguous *other* coming from another continent and another millennium.

Significantly, the opposites are unexpectedly reconciled in the mayor of New York, Rudy Giuliani. He used to be described as skillful but arrogant. Was there a hubris of the mayor that mirrored the hubris of the city? After the tragedy on the morning of September 11, the press could only praise him. He had gone through cancer treatment, a disastrous divorce, and since September 11, through the dust and suffering of "ground zero." What appeared once as an omnipotent psychology in Rudy Giuliani now seems to have integrated the sense of limits, the precariousness of human existence.

There is no doubt that from a psychological point of view the terrorists have scored one point: they wanted to scare the West and they succeeded. They wanted to globalize the Intifada and the attacks of its "Islamic martyrs" and they succeeded. If the consequences of September 11 were to match terrorist wishes, we would witness the ruin of peace not only in Palestine, but globally.

But the West may have recovered something. We may have regained an awareness that we are no substitute for God, that we are not without limits. Nor can we be the agents of God as the terrorists have imagined themselves. This new awareness comes from our wounds and from the unconscious shadow of excess. The terrorists, by contrast, are probably losing rather then acquiring consciousness. They have made their psychological presence felt everywhere, and they risk inflation, possession by a suddenly acquired sense of power, omnipotence. And, as omnipotence came through destructiveness, so destructiveness may become omnipotent. From a practical point of view the terrorists may become blind and make too risky calculations like Hitler after the surprising successes of his Blitzkrieg. From the psychological perspective, possession would mean that the terrorists might extend their violence, lose contact with its meaning, and lose the religious conviction – perverse to us – that motivated them.

The psychic experience of violence tends to reproduce itself endlessly in the victim. This is what we call the trauma experience. But the psychic experience of violence tends to reproduce itself endlessly also in the perpetrator if he falls into the grips of archetypal violence.

The authors of the September 11 attacks were possessed (that is, without a reflective consciousness) by an archetype of divine justice in the form of redeeming violence.[6] Since their possession is personal and unrelated to the surrounding culture and times, the terrorists risk traumatizing themselves through the totalitarian quality of their violence (the paradox is that violence, being "total," destroys not only their psyches but also their bodies).

We can see this same pattern in Macbeth who can only go on killing till he conceives life as "… a tale told by an idiot, full of sound and fury.…" Once irrevocably possessed by violence, the life of Macbeth becomes simply "… full of sound and fury, signifying nothing" (*Macbeth*, V, v 26-28). We can imagine a similar fate for today's fundamentalist terrorists.

III. On Sound and Fury

Front page of *Le Monde Diplomatique*. First article, signed by I. Ramonet, from the first line on:

September 11. Distracted from their normal mission by pilots who decided to risk everything, the planes speed towards the hearth of the great city, ready to destroy the symbols of a hated power.… Explosions … collapses.

---

[6] See Girard, R. *La violence et le sacré* (1972) and *Le bouc émissaire* (1982), Grasset, Paris

Let us not be lost in details because what counts comes a few lines later.

New York 2001? No, Santiago, September 11, 1973.

Now it is really not necessary to go further because we can easily recognize the thesis that underlies this article and other articles covering – extensively, in the October 2001 issue of *Le Monde Diplomatique* – the issue of the terrorist attacks against the U.S. On two occasions the front page repeats: "The U.S. is not an innocent country."

The U.S. administration bears some responsibility for supporting several violent and illegal dictatorial regimes (Batista's Cuba, Pinochet's Chile, Duarte's El Salvador, Somoza's Nicaragua, for example). Is this an answer of the European intellectuals to the attack against the half of the West which lies on the other side of the Atlantic? I must distinguish what I mean by "responsibility." Legal and moral responsibility are personal. (See Jaspers, who distinguishes between a moral and a metaphysical responsibility of the Germans for the Nazi dictatorship).[7] Only in a political, philosophical, or historical sense can a responsibility be extended to a whole social class, to a whole country, a whole civilization. Our psychological point of view starts with the individual but, particularly in the Jungian approach and in this context, can be extended to the collective. This responsibility was basically a novelty introduced during the twentieth century in order not to let German war crimes remain unpunished. The application of collective responsibility is limited, however, and its limits are obvious. The extension of responsibility to the whole German society meant that even the children of heroic opponents, murdered by the Nazi regime, had to pay taxes which supported funds for compensation of the Nazi war crimes.

---

[7] Jaspers, K. *Die Schuldfrage.* Piper, München, 1946

But this extension shows its limits also in the subtle analysis of professional historians. The most well-known "war of historians" is probably the *Historikerstreit* from 1986 that debated the responsibility of Nazism. Spearheading what has been called the "revisionist current," E. Nolte saw the growing destructiveness of Hitler, and in particular of the Nazi "final solution," not as "caused," yet as "psychologically inspired" by previous "Asiatic" genocidal violence that had exploded in Turkey and in the Soviet Union (*Vergangenheit, die nicht vergehen will*, June 6, 1986, *Frankfurter Allgemeine Zeitung*). The ensuing debate was enormous in Germany and outside. The majority accepted in part Nolte's reconstruction, but rejected his attempt to relativize or extenuate the absolute dimension of the Nazi crime.

The clamor of the *Historikerstreit* reminds us that what was at stake was much more than a specialist historiographical analysis. Its psychological and moral implications are enormous and have constituted a kind of milestone. History is infinitely more complex than personal biographies. There is always an antecedent (*Ursprung*, in Nolte's terminology) or a psychological triggering factor of a specific crime. If we apply to all historical precedents the same principle of "extenuating circumstance" that we use in judging individuals, we will journey backwards through the whole of history till Cain who might remain the only subject fully responsible. To link facts to antecedents will remain a legitimate activity of historians and psychologists alike; yet, we should never renounce to judge a criminal act first of all for what it is.

Now let's move to the more specific perspective of this discussion. Following Ernst Nolte and following *Le Monde Diplomatique* but lacking their straightforwardness, many cultivated Europeans, even many colleagues, ask "Yes, but...." The question already misses our tragic occasion to keep the opposites together and avoid psychological imbalance. Only a fraction of a second is reserved for the "yes" while entire debates are reserved for the "but."

"Yes, the events of September 11 are horrible, but – as we want to understand the events psychologically – we should clarify: why is the U.S. so hated?" Of course, there is not one but many reasons – history is not a philanthropic club. A country which has power uses it and is hated for that. But is this really a psychological contribution to the problem? I doubt very seriously that it is. When we start debating American responsibilities outside America and among non-Americans, there is a strong possibility that we are not trying to understand whether there is a reason. We are trying, on the contrary, to find the reason. We analyze under the premise that there must be a reason.

And this assumption, little by little, could become the reawakening of the paranoid projection to which the masses were intentionally led during the persecution of the Jews: "If they are so hated, they must have done something!" "They must have done something" becomes an anti-American European variation of the new blossoming of global paranoid ideas. Many Europeans, of course, share, as part of the whole West, the persecutory expectation of being at any moment potential victims of a global Wrath of God. The other side of the same paranoia leads others to distance themselves from the U.S., fantasizing that the Wrath of God must be uniquely focused on the U.S. Both groups have their reasons, and sometimes the same people experience both paranoid expectations. Fearful thinking is constricted thinking. The oversimplifications of anxious black-white thinking contribute to the uncontrollable globalization of nightmares and delusions.

Psychological understanding is hindered by the burning emotion. The only winner is Osama bin Laden who has managed to infect the world with what originally was his private world of paranoid and grandiose fantasies. His capacity to infect us with bacteria seems to have been widely exaggerated. As I am writing, not only there is no proof that the anthrax-infected letters were mailed by Islamic fundamentalists but there are reasons to believe that this has been the work of a local mind, reviving the Unabomber in form of a "Una-anthrax." What counts here is rather the following: I would gauge that in mid-October 2001, the U.S. TV channels have been broadcasting hours of information dedicated to bacteria for each 10 minutes dedicated to the war in Afghanistan. We had reasons to sense that an infection was coming but, immersed in such an un-psychological world as we are, we have only been able to project the danger and see it in a material, non-psychological form. In this sense, the terrorists have been even more successful because of our post-modern psychic vulnerability. They didn't have to mail poisoned letters. They didn't have to attack the flight AA 587 which crashed in Queens after September 11. Events have occurred by chance as if the terrorists' will were ruling decisive events of our world. Of our inner world?

Our inner world – are we in the end saying that if we look at things psychologically, we should give up the possibility of criticizing past mistakes of the American administration? Not at all. But in order to really elaborate the American psychological issue, the question "Why so much hate against the U.S.?" should be debated first of all among Americans. Of course one can find antecedents. But if we look for "causes," we might become too mechanical. After all, finding out that it was criminal to support the illegal coup by Pinochet is to discover that water is wet. Besides, the attackers of September 11 were Arabs, not Chileans. The problem is not strictly "genetic." We shouldn't expect to see our nemesis necessarily as a genetic continuation, as a revenge of a victim of Pinochet or of one of their orphans. Rather, nemesis can surface wherever there is a corresponding psychological constellation.

In order to be psychological, the link between the terrorists' practices, the practices of the American administration, and the deep reactions of the lay person worldwide, must be searched in terms of meanings and archetypes. Was it an expression of hubris for a superpower to contribute to the illegal and murderous elimination of the legitimately elected president of a much weaker country? Osama bin Laden and the terrorists are a different case, but they exploit the universal – today called "global" – expectation that hubris will be, one day, followed by nemesis.

Being neither lawyers nor generals, we are not in a position to anticipate whether the military actions, or the promised ransom offered for bin Laden, can contribute to the elimination of terrorism. Of course, offering high sums of money can have some effect in desperately poor countries. Being psychologists, though, we wonder to what extent this couldn't also attract Arab sympathy toward the fundamentalists and spur a proud rejection of American money. And of those people close to Osama bin Laden, who could really collaborate toward his capture? Of course, they could count on very high retirement benefits if they were to receive such a ransom. Are people who sacrifice their life without the slightest hesitation really interested in counting on a comfortable third age, a U.S. sponsored retirement plan? Are we sure that this isn't, once again, a miscalculation due to our reductive Western vision?

Osama bin Laden is wealthy yet he has offered not money but Heaven as ransom, and he seems to have been successful. By tempting a traitor with money, the U.S. might score a point but get a short victory. By promoting faith, one can continue the fight endlessly. I am not suggesting that the U.S. should withdraw its ransom but rather that the U.S. should demonstrate some modesty and appropriate pride. Haven't we watched with great respect the mayor of New York sending back a very rich check to an arrogant sheik?

If the U.S. can find ways to turn arrogance into humility, I think it will take a step toward a dramatically new psychological attitude, probably the only one capable of stopping the persecutory scapegoating of everything which is American.

I know that the reality of international affairs is far more complicated than I am suggesting. It is much more difficult to change a collective psychology, and particularly the aspect of the collective psyche which we call culture, than it is to dedicate money to new programs. To change our collective psychology, we must face, first of all, the philosophy which has shaped the ruling circles of the country. This reflection is precisely the interesting possibility. The U.S. has been shaped, probably more than any other country, by pragmatism, that is, by the philosophy of not having a specific philosophy, or, rather, of not having a fixed one, an idealistic or Platonic one. American mobility, before showing up in its geography or social classes, shows up in this education of the mind. Even the word "philosophy" is influenced by this: in Italian, it refers to a theoretical attitude, in English, it also refers to its immediate and practical application.

America, therefore, can revise its attitudes quickly ... if the change is considered better, if it is practical. So, to go back to our psychological theme, America could swiftly change its "hubristic" attitudes if there is a proof – and we believe that it is possible to prove it – that modest attitudes would be both more just and more convenient and effective.

The resistances to a change of attitude will not come only from American circles which might lose power through a more modest attitude (merchants of arms, for instance); the resistance might come from all other countries with a different prevailing philosophy, countries much more wary of change. These countries typically label the U.S. as a cynical country with no faith, no ideals, no God, only a preoccupation with material gains. In such countries pragmatism is a psychological attitude which has not been developed. Being unconscious, pragmatism becomes an occasion for a collective shadow projection. The flexibility of American politics is seen by non-pragmatic or idealistic cultures as an expression of greed and a lack of morality. American flexibility, however, can well express itself as the long awaited modesty, as a capacity to pragmatically recognize one's errors.

Despite its potential, American pragmatism and flexibility in politics contribute to its frequent astonishing lack of foresight and psychological sensitivity. Without resorting to the usual examples of U.S. policies in Latin-America, let me simply mention my country. The U.S. acquired in Italy an enormous respect because many of its soldiers haddied on our shores, helping us to get rid of Fascism and Nazism. Not even the most violent anti-American propaganda really denied this because soon after conquering our soil, American troops went back home and were substituted for by economical help (the Marshall Plan).

Yet, in the decades following World War II, uncontrollable hands in the American administration on several occasions gave help to neo-fascist, illegal, and violent groups within Italy. The alleged purpose seems to have been an attempt to counter the growing influence of the PCI (Italian Communist Party). It is not our task to evaluate if this bent for intrigue was political stupidity, but we may wonder what the widows and orphans of American soldiers who fell in the fight against Fascism may think of the fact that in the 1950s the U.S. administration supported some Italian neo-fascist groups. It is easy to document that the Italian collective psychology was highly influenced by American intrusions which ultimately brought large gains to the PCI, the exact opposite of American purposes.

America has the great capacity of being capable of redirecting its international policies in a short time. Yet, it will then have to accept the "coexistence of the opposites" in philosophies. It will have to accept that other countries have a different relationship with flexibility. If the U.S. will change its attitude to a more modest one – a change to its advantage I think – it will have to proceed without asking for immediate recognition of the new "virtuous" attitude.

All in all, American international politics have often been so pragmatically flexible as to damage severely its own image. The U.S. has been so interested in tactics (short term advantages) as to go against its strategic (longer term) interests. More than this, its politics have been flexible with disregard for the opinion of other populations – which is to say, nonchalant with hubris. And the offended populations often find, with a malignant smile, frequent confirmations that it was hubris indeed. As we have recalled, the punishment of hubris – nemesis – loves to make "U-turns" and use the very instrument of arrogance to punish the arrogant. Like the Sorcerer's Apprentice who lost control of his magical helpers, the U.S. has had to face the many brutal dictators or warlords who turned against their "benefactor." None of them, though, has backfired with such sound and fury as Osama bin Laden.

We have continued to come back to the problem of union and division of the archetypal polarities. Let us talk about union and division in a country and among countries in collective psychology. What Europeans seldom seem to understand is that the "U" of "U.S.A." doesn't stand just for an adjective – "United" – it stands also for a philosophy and a faith. After September 11, we witnessed on television the obsessive repetition of "America" and "American," each occurrence reiterating the fight of Good against Evil and at the same time the fight of Union against Division. It is very difficult to explain this to Europeans. All of the flag waving, the talk of "our Nation," and the repetition of "America" corresponds to *a conscious desire for unity*. As an European it is really possible to understand this desire for unity only if you live in the U.S. and your children go to an American school.

For Europeans, division was experienced in its worst form in war, and war originated in nationalism. This is particularly true for those countries that experienced a dictatorship in addition to war. In the second half of September 2001, I heard in the U.S. the expressions "Nation" and "American" many, many more times than I ever heard the corresponding "nazione" and "italiano/a" (words which in our language are not capitalized) in 57 years of life in Italy. Basically, "nazione" was Mussolini's vocabulary, and nowadays only the post-fascist party qualifies itself as "Nazionale." In the German vocabulary, the adjective, "national," has practically survived only in the word "Nazi." Only in the U.S. is nationalism meant to underline *equality and not difference*, union and not division. Because of its size and because of the absence, particularly nowadays, of visible enemies at its borders, the U.S. debate is turned inwards, basically to internal and not to international issues.

We constantly hear that the American administration pays attention to the psychological aspect of international affairs and that it recruits many psychologists for this task. It would be valuable if the psychologists were to remind the administration that the U.S. is, in this as in many issues, the exception: "national" implies more often external conflict rather than internal unity. A nation and its nationalistic issues are, as a rule, defined by confrontation with other nations. There is no way to escape the international dimension, even for the U.S. since English is – fortunately or unfortunately – the international language. Therefore, U.S. media is the media of the world; CNN is the voice of the news for the whole of the West and for the whole world. As a consequence, when CNN broadcasts the word "nation" worldwide, it doesn't only promote union but also division, not only equality but also difference.

CNN's constant headline, "America's New War," little by little created a disaffection among those Europeans who initially identified with the U.S. and with the tragedy of September 11. The phrase reinforced the crawling cynicism of those who say: "It is not our business." And, of course, it was a delight for Osama bin Laden who, long since, has had the declared objective of singling out the U.S. and blaming it for the evil of the world.

What are we to understand when America's official voices tell us that the terrorists hate the U.S. because it is a country acting under the rule of the law and who then invoke "Wild West" and call for Osama bin Laden "dead or alive"? Psychologically, the language of the "wild west" alienates all Europeans who, in spite of being on the average less religious than Americans, believe that God and not man is the administrator of death. Logically, "dead or alive" sacrifices the consistency which is the essence of the rule of law where punishment is decided only by the court. Even if one supports capital punishment, it is wrong to kill first and then hold a trial.

Are all of the psychological advisors of the American administration on leave in such a delicate moment? Why do the official speakers always include "American" when they describe the terrorists as criminals who kill "innocent American civilians" or "innocent American children"? Don't they notice that, translated into a language other than English, "innocent American children" sounds strange, as though "innocent children" are somehow different. In any other language one who kills innocents is a criminal, independently of the nationality of the victim.

American politicians are elected by the American voters, yet this is a universal condition, valid wherever there are democratic elections. Elsewhere U.S. politicians speak naturally of "human rights," not just of "American rights." Besides, from the point of view of international relations the U.S. has a global responsibility like no other country and in no other moment of history. Indeed, the U.S. has an international responsibility not only today, as the only superpower, but, so-to-say, genetically. Unlike other countries, which were born locally and remained local, U.S. politics were declared international from the very first lines of its first document, the Declaration of Independence. The United States declared that it would "... assume among the powers of the earth, the separate and equal station to which the Laws of Nature and Nature's God entitle them...."

Once again, as psychologists, we wonder if the U.S. administration has at its disposal colleagues reminding it that slogans have not only an immediate effect but also a lasting, unconscious, and potentially corrosive psychological effect? Expressions like "infinite justice" or "they have awakened a mighty giant" recall a psychic condition of omnipotence – such arrogance and hubris can gradually alienate the rest of the world.

The conquest of the sky has always been an American endeavor. From the short leap of the Wright brothers, to Lindberg, to John Glenn, Neil Armstrong, and the other astronauts, America has been attracted to the sky through flight as well as through the construction of sky-scrapers as if it possessed a specific, reversed force of gravity. Flying has been an American temptation, an American glory, and at the same time an American hubris. Even the melancholic figure of J.J. Kennedy wasn't exempt from it, when he left for his final flight to Martha's Vineyard, neglecting a reasonable respect for limits.

Once again, it is not the psychologist's task to evaluate whether from a military perspective it makes sense to send planes to Afghanistan, each of which costs a significant portion of Afghanistan's yearly income. It is the psychologist's task to discuss to the *psychological* cost of the bombing, particularly in relation to the economic one, and in relation to its historical cost. Nobody has forgotten that the U.S. dropped more bombs on Vietnam than it dropped in the whole of Europe in World War II, yet in the end the U.S. had to leave Vietnam. It seems natural to think that the memory of Vietnam, the excess of hubris, and the loss of prestige would discourage the U.S. military from taking similar risks today. Unfortunately, the priority given to air attacks comes from reasons linked not only with strategy, but also with internal politics. More than any other military power, the U.S. tries to beat the enemy from afar in order to avoid casualties. The inspiring principle would be, of course, respectable and even humanitarian if it weren't for the fact that U.S. military casualties tend to be reduced at the cost of an enormous increase of casualties among the enemy's civilian (that is, more or less, innocent) population.

Air power has been a more and more firm policy throughout time. Its first mass application took place during World War II ("carpet bombing"). Its military effectiveness has been widely discussed; in Italy, and particularly in Germany and Japan, although air strikes disrupted communications and military production, military factories were relocated many times. The moribund Fascist and Nazi propaganda recovered new life by describing – for once without much necessity to lie – the air war as particularly "cruel" and "cowardly" (the latter adjective, by a strange coincidence or nemesis, was used in the American response to the terrorists who were hideously cruel but not cowardly).

We should wonder if the psychological aspect of this one-sidedness – repeated in Vietnam, in Kosovo, and now in Afghanistan – has been evaluated. The polarities are separated physically, visually: "Evil below, good above." In the long run, the split creates the image of two classes of separated humans: superior people who should never die and inferior people who can die or survive without really living until their time comes. Is military necessity always the decisive necessity? Wouldn't we agree with the necessity of avoiding the imaginal division of humans in two: "those above" and "those below"? Isn't there some psychological necessity to avoid images which contradict the founding principle of the U.S. "that all men are created equal"?

From a point of view which is, unfortunately, imaginal as well as Clausewitzian, bombing is the military continuation of politics which define the enemy as "evil." Bombs represent the last military stage of the politics of oversimplification, the politics of psychological splitting, of division. Such politics fall into the fundamentalist trap which defines the enemy as evil, as Satan – the same politics that foster Islamic attacks on the West. Today's rhetoric encourages the globalization of "sound and fury." The risk of radically antagonizing the opposites, of using absolute, non-analyzable terms such as "evil" is that in the end, as the journalist N. Solomon said, we might simply have "evil against evil."

It is extremely difficult to say something that may last. As a psychologist, I feel that I have condemned myself to criticizing certain things without suggesting positive alternatives. I would like to say: "Don't rebuild the Twin Towers! Leave 'Ground Zero' as a memorial, as food for a necessary memory of the destruction. Let us accept the scar, the sadness, without reverting immediately and totally to one-sided optimism." But, what do I know of the needs of urban planning, of architecture, of finance? I can only say that the reconstruction of the Twin Towers is, or could be, an act of hubris. The possible allegation of hubris has been and still is a dangerous and potentially devastating threat hanging over the U.S.

Bombs – of course, those of the terrorists are also bombs, although they nominally used planes – separate and polarize the opposites. Bombs remain over time and not only metaphorically: Not long ago I was blocked in traffic in my home city, Milan, together with some ten thousand people because a huge unexploded bomb dropped by the Allied forces in 1944 had been unearthed during an excavation. "Sound and fury," once dropped on us, remain in the subterranean parts of the psyche, never exploding for good. Having more experience with bombs from the sky, undetonated bombs, and terrorist attacks (the Red Brigade, IRA, and Bader-Meinhof, for example), Europeans have unique historical perspectives to contribute to the dialogue across the Atlantic. Europeans, therefore, have compelling reasons to join Americans in conversations about hope and terror, hubris and nemesis, the West and the not-West, recalling that the "West" exists in American, European, global, and local versions.

Luigi Zoja is a diplomate of the C.G. Jung Institute, Zurich, and past president of the IAAP (International Association of Analytical Psychology). He practiced in Zurich, then in Milan and at present is located in New York State. His books in English include: *The Father*, Routledge, London, 2001; *Drugs, Addiction and Initiation*, 2nd ed. Daimon, Einsiedeln, 2000; *Growth and Guilt*, Routledge, London and New York, 1995.

Islamic Terrorism

Wolfgang Giegerich

I want to preface the following remarks with two quota-
tions. The first is from Goethe and was meant as a warning
against the inflated emotionalism/irrationalism of the
Romantics. It reads, "The Germans should not use the word
Gemüt [soul, heart, the seat of large-scale, warm emotions, the
inner world in its totality] for a period of thirty years; then by
and by *Gemüt* might restore itself again." Applied to our
situation this statement might read, "The Jungians would do
well not to use the words 'the numinous' and 'the sacred' for a
period of thirty years."[1] The second quotation is from Aristotle
and reads, "It is a sign of *apaideusía* (lack of cultural refine-
ment) not to know for what a proof has to be sought and for
what not" (*Met.* 1006 a 6). Adjusting this insight to our context
we could say, "It is a sign of *apaideusía* not to know for which
phenomena the archetypal perspective is called for and for
which not." Psychology has to resist the temptation to inflate
with archetypal or mythical significance events, dream

---

[1] I leave off the continuation to be expected on the basis of the Goethean
sentence, since I doubt that today in the case of the "numinous" and the
"sacred" there could be a restoration analogous to the one Goethe envisioned as possible with respect to "Gemüt." Rather, it seems that the time of
the "numinous" in the proper sense of the word is over, the inflated,
ideological use made of the term in some quarters being one of the symptoms of its demise as a psychological reality.

images, and emotional reactions stemming from our personal or collective complexes or from plain social and political conditions. It has to learn to discriminate; what empirically is spectacular, huge, sensational, may nevertheless be psychologically commonplace or even banal, and what, by contrast, is psychologically of deepest significance may well be empirically unobtrusive. We could also say psychology has to learn to discriminate between what authentically belongs to the sphere of practical reality and the "psychology of the ego" on the one hand, and what is expressive of a movement in the "hinterland of the soul," on the other.

This is why in these reflections I will ignore the dramatic events of September 11, 2001. They do not need special *psychological* attention. There have been other disasters with more dead persons in recent history (Ruanda, Kosovo, etc.); acts of terrorism have been with us for decades; it was not a surprise that America was the target of terrorist attacks; that there is no guarantee of safety is a familiar insight. Rather than focussing on one particular event I will try to think about the phenomenon of Islamic terrorism at large with the special question in mind of how we should assess it.

"True" versus Real *Islam*

There have been and still are terrorist groups in many places. Mostly they are small and to be understood in terms of a local situation. But Islamic terrorism stands out – not only because of its focus of hatred against the United States of America and because of its extensive, almost global network and its technical sophistication, but also because of the enormous moral backing it has in large sections of the populations of Islamic countries (including large parts of the intelligentsia). The designation "Islamic" seems to be appropriate. This terrorism is a peculiarly Islamic phenomenon. Such passionate hatred directed against America is for the most part lacking in Black Africa or in non-Islamic Asia, or even in Vietnam where anger against America might be considered much more likely for historical reasons. We cannot merely charge a small group of misguided people with interpreting their terrorism as an Islamic jihad against infidels. The connection with Islam is, at least to some extent, intrinsic.

Many Islam scholars and many well-meaning people in the West warn against confusing the acts and ideology of the Islamic terrorists with Islam as such. True Islam, they claim, is a peaceful religion, and the "jihad," they point out, actually has a strictly religious meaning very different from the way the terrorists use the term. As justified as this caution is academically, it is also irrelevant, even misleading, in the concrete situation we are in and as regards an attempt to understand what is going on. It does not make sense to work with the trick of a radical separation of different aspects, by attributing everything good and pious to a so-called "true Islam" and everything bad to an "inauthentic (or misunderstood) Islam" and switching from the one to the other as convenient. This merely obscures the issue and legitimizes the equivocal use of the word "Islam" by the two groups. Three facts have to be noted. (1) Those terrorists profess themselves Moslems; they speak and act in the name of Islam and for its higher glory. (2) The general public in the Islamic world does not unmistakably and categorically dissociate itself from the terrorists and from their claim to act in the name of Islam. (3) There are even enough preachers in mosques, enough Islamic religious leaders who openly appeal to hatred and in doing so remain uncontradicted and uncondemned. What the terrorist do thus reflects on Islam as such; maybe indeed not on "true (authentic, original) Islam as it *should* be understood," but certainly on *real Islam*.

The Breeding Ground of Terrorism

It has been suggested that the terrorists are the voice of the poor and humiliated masses, the losers in the changes brought about by globalization. The poor themselves are not self-assured, educated and experienced enough to be able to express and fight for their own interests, let alone plan and carry out sophisticated terrorist attacks. So individual people from the educated and well-off middle or upper class stand up in their stead, as their advocates and avengers, taking upon themselves the cause of the masses. Therefore, even though the protagonists of terrorism are sons of rich fathers, the actual roots of Islamic terrorism are to be sought in the slums. The terrorists act on behalf of the poor. They have the higher mission to call attention to gross, but ignored injustices, a mission that derives its authority from an unspoken mandate of the masses.

This view, it seems to me, is totally mistaken. The terrorists are not the mouthpiece of the poor, are not the defenders of their cause. Present Islamic terrorism does not have its origin below, in the misery and longings of the masses. The breeding ground of terrorism is the abstract intellect. It comes from on top. It is a brain child, ideological. From what one hears, it seems that Usama bin Laden for one has downright contempt for the masses. At any rate terrorism is not rooted in the material misery of the people as its soil. No Robin Hood romanticism. The terrorists are mentally detached from the people (although they may believe to be, and give themselves the appearance of, representing them). Never themselves having led the life of the poor masses and never having felt their kind of worries, they don't know the real poor and their needs, their suffering, and have no real connection with them, which does not exclude the possibility that they relate to their own fantasy images of them. What motivates terrorists and "authorizes" them are top-heavy, abstract principles, on the one hand, and their own complicated inner being, their tangled subjectivities, on the other. They are idealists, totally obedient to, indeed obsessed by, certain *ideas* (just as were the anarchists, the Marxist-Leninists and others during the first half of the 20th century).

But this idealism of theirs is purely negative, destructive. It is exclusively a fight *against* (the "Great Devil" America or the West). There are no constructive ideas, no utopian visions of a better society, no plans for building up a new world after the destruction of the old one. No thoughts are wasted by the Islamic terrorists on concrete help for their countries or on curing the most pressing social ills. The entire concentration is on the goal of annihilating the Great Devil and the infidels, and this purely negative goal seems to be an absolute *end in itself*. There is, though, one positive value that they fight *for*: Allah, the true faith. But *their* Allah obviously is himself only an abstract *immediate* negation[2], nothing positive, and he seems to be no more than the objectified (hypostatized) personification of the their own will to destruction.

Because the will to annihilate is unconditional, Western thinking, which is heir to the tradition of the Enlightenment, has great difficulty finding a place in its scheme of things for the phenomenon of terrorism. The enlightened mind, as Jürgen Kaube pointed out[3], is able to imagine reasonable emotions or affects: the feelings of injustice, outrage, impatience. It cannot really fathom the affects that drive the terrorists: envy, resentment and hatred. They are unthinkable. Those other emotions (injustice, outrage and so on, and similarly fear and self-interest) are still committed to and guided by the idea of some good. Not so the affects of the terrorists. What they are committed to is negation absolute.

---

[2] In contrast to a mediated negation, the negation of the negation.
[3] In *Frankfurter Allgemeine Zeitung*, 8 Nov. 2001, p. 45.

Possessed by the emotions of envy and hatred, one *does not want* improvement for oneself, does not want practical solutions; one is satisfied if the situation of others worsens. This confirms the above thesis that terrorism originates in a sphere diametrically opposed to that where the real worries of practical, day to day life are felt: in a sphere of abstract principles. Principles are absolute, they are derived through purification, through abstraction from all contamination with sensual and pragmatic concerns. Whereas principles such as human rights, justice, freedom normally have concrete human benefits as their goal, the principle of terrorism is principle to the power of two, principleness absolute, for principleness' sake: negation as such, the stripping *per se* from all material, pragmatic concerns and purposes. The only true absolute is absolute negation. Anything the least bit positive is ipso facto relative. With the terrorists the bond normally attaching each person to the material interests of creaturely man has been severed; which is, by the way, one reason why they are willing to consider their own perishing.

If Islamic terrorists are not representatives or advocates of the common people, there is nevertheless an element of representation in their fight, but on the opposite side, the side of the enemy to be attacked. Islamic terrorism is, as it were, a proxy war. Actually the hatred and discontent of the "sons" is meant for their own (not personal) "fathers," the repressive regimes. But "the West" has to stand in as a bogeyman. They blame the West, but mean the political system in their own countries, of course completely unconsciously. So although the terrorists are disconnected from the practical down-to-earth interests of the common people and although terrorism has its source in abstract ideas, this move away from the material base of real social interests to the sphere of an abstract intellect is nevertheless itself rooted in and brought forth by the very real social conditions in which the persons who became terrorists grew up. The general climate in most of the Islamic countries is such that people have no prospects for the future, neither individually, nor collectively, and especially not intellectually, with respect to a free unfolding of the needs of the mind. The mind is stifled. For young, intelligent persons not immediately absorbed by the daily practical struggle for existence and receptive to the invisible atmosphere of the real situation, there is a feeling of hopelessness and meaninglessness of existence as such (Nietzsche: "What is wanting is a goal. What is wanting is an answer to the 'What for?' "). This general feeling in combination with the all too real experience that their own social situation is an impasse creates the longing for an *absolute* goal: Because the concrete reality experienced in their home countries does not even afford the possibility of the *vision* of a satisfying future, the "libido" is altogether driven away from a striving for positive ends in reality and up into the sphere of abstract principles in their most extreme form, the principle of destruction absolute.

C.G. Jung captured this existential situation pretty well when he said (in a different connection): People "are simply sick of the whole thing, sick of that banal life, and therefore they want sensation. They even want a war; they all want a war. They are all glad when there is a war: they say, 'Thank heaven, now something is going to happen – something bigger than ourselves!'" (CW 18 § 627)

The otherworldly, extramundane character of the terrorists' idealism lends itself to, or even requires, its self-interpretation in terms of religion. While the terrorists ostensibly fall back on their traditional religion, Islam, it is a religion which has become transplanted from its home ground in the soul into the icy world of absolutely abstract principles. It becomes fundamentalistic: religious ideology.

The Predicament of Islam and the Islamic World

As all religions today, so Islam, too, is obsolete, no longer adjusted to present-day reality. It does not correspond to the status of consciousness that has been reached and prevails in the world. It is not in tune with the way human reality is constituted today. Religion simply does not grip anymore. It runs idle, as a mere *supplement* to life.

This is not what religion was meant to be. Once upon a time religion was the highest and most comprehensive articulation of the truth of human reality. It was capable of expressing the otherwise inaccessible logical or psychological *depth* of actually lived life. It was up to date, state of the art, at the forefront of human development, even pointing ahead to the future, inspiring new developments. But today, religion – with respect to its highest determination – is a thing of the past; it has nothing to contribute to the great issues of the age; the authority for truth has devolved upon science, the media, etc. Even if he has not always consciously noticed it subjectively, objectively man has outgrown religion today. It functions only as a private embellishment of life, as a spiritual spare-time entertainment, a commodity for sale on the market for "meaning," not as the *known* truth of the age and the *universal, public* truth of a people.

Even if the Islamic world does not admit it and to a large extent perseveres in a medieval frame-of-mind, factually it has long been living in the modern world. The only way religion could *legitimately* survive under the conditions of modernity would be if it were transformed into an objectively non-committal private affair of the individual. If religion, if Islam is, however, held on to as a publicly binding creed despite these fundamental changes, it comes into conflict with the truth of the age. And because it is no longer true (the articulation of the inner truth and depth of life as it is actually lived and constituted), no longer simply speaking for itself, this lack of objective truth must be compensated for, with respect to its internal logical form, by a rigid, authoritarian dogmaticism (fundamentalism), on the one hand, and, with respect to the relation of the subject to his or her own belief, by an excess of subjective affect and will (fanaticism), on the other. It becomes regressive, falling back behind itself, thus turning more primitive than it originally was, cruder, more violent, and sclerotic.

Besides the fact that religion at large is disengaged from where life is today, there is an additional problem that Islam has to contend with. Once Islam was at the spearhead of cultural development. During the early Middle Ages it was culturally far ahead of Europe in many regards. But for several centuries it has been at a standstill. There has been no further development. The great progressive thinkers, mystics, poets of the Islamic word of the Middle Ages and later were not able to prevail over rigid orthodoxy, which ultimately always remained victorious. This is why Islam, to express it with a sweeping statement, has nothing to offer today with respect to the great questions of the age, neither intellectually, nor economically, nor politically. All the important impulses and achievements come from the West.

The present moral, political, economic, intellectual superiority of the Western world creates a deep-seated collective inferiority feeling in the Islamic world, all the more so because of the formerly justified, today false claim to be a leading culture. This inferiority feeling also feeds the terrorists. Now it is crucial to understand that the experienced inferiority is met by a consciousness informed by a "shame culture." The Islamic soul feels humiliated, shamed. Shame as the violation of one's honor is an extremely powerful emotion, pretty much unknown in the modern West, in which the place of the *vital, ethnic* and *substantiated* value of personal or national *honor* is taken by the *abstract legal* idea of *human dignity* as such. Shame usually requires revenge as a reaction in order to restore the violated honor. This is why the terrorists' idealism is (has to be) purely negative, destructive: the restoration of one's lost honor requires the death of the humiliator and not the betterment of one's own condition, not any practical advantage. It may even include the obligation to sacrifice one's own life (suicide bombers), "honor" being a value absolutely superior to "life" or "existence," while in civilizations governed by the idea of human dignity as their highest value there is the contrary tendency to consider the intactness of the "person(ality)" required by this value to also include the necessity to protect the intact physical existence (i.e., life) of each empirical person. Here in the West, to exist (no matter how) therefore tends to become an *absolute* value which in ethnic shame cultures would be incomprehensible.

The Western world does not only subjectively feel superior. It is objectively superior, and not merely because of its cultural achievements and economic power, but also in its *internal constitution*. Its superiority is founded on the fact that it is logically more complex in a way similar to how a multicellular organism is superior to a protozoon: the Western mind has taken several developmental steps and thereby continually differentiated itself: in difficult, painful struggles it pushed off from itself (from itself as "Middle Ages"); it overcame itself repeatedly on ever new levels. Through such movements as the Reformation, the religious wars, the Inquisition against heretics and witches, the overcoming of the Inquisition, and the Enlightenment it sort of cut into its own flesh. It subjected its religion, its traditional customs, its history, its values to a fundamental historical, scientific, and philosophical critique.

An equivalent development of a self-sublation and rising above itself did not take place in the Islamic world, where continued work upon a critical reflection of its own religion, tradition, social reality has not been undertaken. It has not dissolved the naive, unbroken unity with itself, its *participation mystique* with its own religion. The critical fight with, indeed *against itself* and its own orthodoxy has not taken place. Islam has not attempted to within itself distance itself from itself so as to be able to see itself as if from outside. Rather, it remains in a (cultural) "nature" stage, as, for example, the undiminished prevalence of the ancient emotions of shame and honor (as substantial, almost "physical" realities) as well as such phrases as "our Islamic brothers" or the notion of the Islamic *umma* (one single "nation" of believers, set off from all other peoples) indicate. Although "brothers" does not refer to natural, literal brothers, but is used metaphorically, this metaphor uses the idea of a natural blood relationship and therefore transports (*metapherein*) thinking in terms of natural conceptions to the level of religion, reaffirming the "nature" stage of consciousness even on that level. *Mutatis mutandis* the same could be said about the *umma*. The immediate family, clan, or tribe has been overcome, but only to be replaced by the large spiritual "tribe" of all believers. The *umma* refers to the concretistic unity of *natural* persons, distinguished from others by the *empirical (positive) feature* of their being adherents to Islam. In other words, Islam has not yet risen above a tribal consciousness to the abstraction of "man as such" and of human rights. It is in this light that a statement attributed to bin Laden has to be seen, the statement that before God the suppression of a single Moslem outweighs the destruction of the whole world.

So my speaking of the superiority of the West does not refer to *contents*, but to the *logical form or status of consciousness*, its degree of differentiation and complexity. I am by no means claiming that contentwise Islam is inferior to or "worse" than, e.g., Christianity. I am not comparing and evaluating the respective spiritual teachings of these two religions or cultures. In fact we are past that stage in which "content" was the decisive criterion and main interest. What counts today is the logical level that has been achieved. And in this regard, a comparison between the Christian West and the Islamic world shows a considerable differential.

The talk of a "clash of civilizations" tends to obscure the essential problem by creating the impression that the two civilizations here in question are located *on the same level*. But the real conflict is not between two religions, Islam and Christianity, nor between a religious civilization and a secular one, nor between two geographic regions (East and West). Rather it is a conflict between two civilizations separated by a temporal, historical gap: the conflict between "Middle Ages" and "Modernity," as two logical stages of consciousness. Of course, one could try to conceive of Middle Ages and Modernity as two options (to cultural styles) side by side despite the fact that time separates them (and us from the Middle Ages) objectively, but this does not work because Modernity is in itself the sublated, overcome Middle Ages. In other words, the temporal gap is at the same time a logical one.

This is precisely why the West is experienced as so threatening by fundamentalist Moslems. It is not so much the political and economic power nor the actual behavior of Western countries toward Islamic states that most deeply troubles the Islamic soul. Rather, it is the dim but correct sense that Western civilization as such, prior to having done anything in particular, *is* the embodied logical negation of the medieval frame-of-mind informing present-day Islam. The mere existence of Western civilization is the constant reminder of Islam's omitted self-reflection and self-critique and of the impending internal logical negation that would necessarily result from such a self-reflection. This is in the last analysis why the West is "The Great Devil" that, in the eyes of the terrorists, simply needs to be extinguished.

The fact that the influence of the West with its capitalism, technology, industry and science, abstract idea of law, tourism and consumerism, "digitalization," feminism and sexual freedom, etc. also more practically means the annihilation of traditional social structures and values, is merely the concretization of the fundamental logical threat. Indeed, the values of a life organized around ethnic and personal relations and traditional customs cannot persist nor can traditional societies' closeness to nature that conveys a sense of embeddedness in the world. The ensuing signs of disintegration, the alienation, the feeling of homelessness in the world, the arbitrariness resulting from an open society, not to mention the loss of male power and the possible resultant loss of economic power of the male part of society due to the emancipation of women naturally create fundamental anxieties and, by way of defense, the moral condemnation of the Western life-style as "decadent," "perverse," the Western world at large as inhabited by "infidels."

Such fears are not to be found exclusively among Islamic people. There are enough opponents of globalization even in the West who share some of these anxieties and judgments with the Islamic fundamentalists and terrorists.

The Implications of and Response to the Inferiority Felt

The experience of one's own inferiority generally implies the necessity to constructively overcome it. The simple fact of its encounter with the modern Western world as a logically – in its internal constitution – more complex world presents Islam with a responsibility, the obligation to do its homework, in order to achieve an equivalent logical differentiation. The job is not imitation, nor the importation of Western culture. It is the task of a thorough-going and patient attempt to intellectually come to terms with the West. First it is the task of positively accepting the obvious differential between the Western and the Islamic worlds as a challenge; it is secondly and above all the task to go through an equivalent process of critical self-reflection in order to thereby bring itself, under its own steam and on its own ground, up to date and thus to become truly creative once more. In one sense the jihad against "the perverse Western world" and against "the infidels" proclaimed by Islamists everywhere is analogue to the religious wars, the fanatic persecution of heretics, and the burning of witches that we had in Europe centuries ago.[4] Or rather it is the analogue to an even earlier stage, that of the Crusades, which was the very beginning of the long European process of the integration of "the Other."[5] The Islamic world is still in the stage of historical development that the West has overcome long ago. The critical struggle with its own orthodoxy, the job of overcoming itself through a process of self-reflection and self-sublation still remains to be shouldered by Islam. But generally, this job has been neglected in the Islamic world; even more than neglected: it has been and is being replaced by stubborn reliance on its glorious past on the one hand, and by making a bogeyman out of the West, who can then be blamed for one's own misery, on the other. What could be a productive challenge is turned into hatred, rage, the will for destruction. Here it is helpful to see how differently,

[4] Just as a number of very different factors and motivations combined to make the historical phenomenon of the Inquisition possible (religious zeal, political interests, personal psychological problems, greed for power and money) and as the fervor of the Inquisition thus had the character of a "feeling-toned complex," so the jihad of the terrorists today of course combines within itself multiple impulses.

[5] Cf. W. Giegerich, "Zuerst Schatten, dann Anima. Oder: Die Ankunft des Gastes. Schattenintegration und die Entstehung der Psychologie," in: *GORGO 15/1988*, pp. 5-28. English: "The Advent of the Guest: Shadow Integration and the Rise of Psychology," in: *Spring 51* (1991), pp. 86-106.

productively Eastern Asia (Japan, Taiwan, Korea, and now China ...) reacted to the encounter with the West.

The Lebanese poet Abbas Baydoun seems to think along similar lines."Even if our reproach that America exploits our suffering and our ineptitude may not be wrong, we nevertheless do not summon an equivalent effort to recognize our own responsibility for the reasons of this suffering. It is a responsibility that increases every day. We have always preferred to nurture a small tyrant inside of each of us who defers any accountability towards ourselves and towards others, until the historical revenge on the West be accomplished – as little hope as may exist for this." "Possibly many among us pray that the racism of the West and the American paranoia may increase, for in this way we would have another excuse for not looking into the mirror. In this way we could again submerge into the delusional idea of a collective suppression, in order to spare ourselves the sight of a dreadful face, the face of another Islam, the Islam of isolation and arbitrary violence which gradually gains the upper hand and soon, as we head for the climax of our delusion, will have become our actual face."[6]

It is so much easier to resort to resentments and blame others for the unsatisfactory condition one find's oneself in than to do one's homework, so much easier to resort to simple slogans and simple answers to complex questions than to engage in a long-term and detailed intellectual struggle with the problems posed by the existence of the modern world, so much easier to act out (throwing bombs) than to *erinnern* (to interiorize, integrate). The terrorists at any rate prefer fanaticism to intellectual labor, prefer building someone else up into a hate object worthy of destruction to working upon *"themselves"*: upon their own religion, cultural tradition and political conditions.

[6] Abbas Baydoun, "Unser Wahn. Die Krise arabischer Intellektueller," in: *FAZ* No. 261, 9 Nov. 2001, p. 45, my translation.

Fanaticism is a "substitutive formation" much in the
Freudian sense. Logically, it is, as pointed out above, the
substitution of excessive subjective affect and will for the
lacking "objective" truth[7] of one's belief-system, and practically it is the substitution of one's acting out for the omitted
and refused obligation to do one's homework. On a personal
level, it amounts to a kind of brain-washing. Something is
broken in the personality. It is no longer alive, open, flexible,
no longer human in the full sense of the word, but functions
monomaniacally like a programmed machine. "When a soldier has fought or even murdered in a war, he becomes tired
at some point; at some point he wants to go home again. This
means, each person who speaks for himself cannot be a
permanent terrorist, a permanent murderer. The Atta's and
bin Laden's, however, function differently – in them the life
and flux of one's feelings has been interrupted so that these
feelings turn into missiles"[8] (Alexander Kluge).

Why America?

It is remarkable that public hatred time and again and
rather onesidedly finds its favorite object in the United States.
This was so even during the times of the cold war when the
Soviet Union could have served with equal right as a hated
enemy for people in the Third World as well as for the
followers of the peace movement in the West. Strangely
enough, there have not been any considerable anti-Russian
demonstrations on account of Chechnia, either. It is always

[7] I want to remind the reader that my speaking of a "lacking truth" refers only
to the discrepancy existing between the form of one's subjective belief-
system and the form of modern consciousness as an objective reality. I am
not making any statement about the contents of any religion or belief-
system *in abstracto*.

[8] "Krieg oder Karambolage? Gespräch mit dem Schriftsteller und Regisseur
Alexander Kluge," in: *Stuttgarter Zeitung* No. 258, 2001.

America that is the target of rage. This suggests a resentment of what America as country and culture stands for; a resentment that is not caused by any particular questionable political or military actions performed by the United States, but rather directed at the *idea* "America" as such. Here we have to ask specifically why there is such a passionate hatred toward America not only on the part of the Islamic terrorist, but also of large sections of the masses in Islamic countries. Although America was never a full-fledged colonial powers in Arab regions, much more hatred is directed against America than against France or Great Britain, which both have been colonial masters in this part of the world.

One reason may be that America as the spearhead of progress and modernity, the most dynamic and productive society, also has to take the full brunt of the resentment born out of the Islamic inferiority feeling we discussed.

Another reason might be that Arab hatred for America is based on the traditional Arab hatred for the Jews. America usually almost unconditionally supports Israel, and the American establishment and administration is heavily exposed to Jewish influence. New York is the city with the greatest Jewish population in the world. Anti-Semitism gives an additional charge to the feelings of hatred existing anyway and is possibly responsible for mythicizing America into the "Great Devil": it is well possible that Anti-Semitism is what explains the religious-numinous quality of the terrorist's jihad against America. This numinous quality might in turn help to explain the willingness of so many terrorists to serve as suicide bombers.

The rage against America is to some extent also caused by its opposite, an idealization of America, on account of which it is measured by far higher and stricter standards than any other country. America is not only the only superpower and a fantastic success story, it is also a country that both professes

freedom, liberty, democracy, human rights as its supreme
values and represents these values also for people in other
countries who often project their longings upon America. The
fact that the policies of the United States often enough contradict this idealized image is a terrible disappointment. One
never forgives one's model if it falls short of one's expectations. Partly, the policies of the United States are short-sighted
or half-hearted, partly they violate publicly avowed principles
for the benefit of ideological or egotistical economic advantages; America has supported corrupt, authoritarian regimes
as well as supplied dubious rebellious groups with weapons
and land mines, causing great misery for the general population.

What Should the Western Reaction Be?

Very generally speaking, the response to Islamic terrorism
has to be twofold; (a) internally, the West has to accept the
challenge posed by Islamic terrorism and do *its* homework;
(b) externally, it has to defend what it stands for.

The homework to be done includes rectification of the
injustice to Palestinians (e.g., the violation of various UN
resolutions and the constant humiliation and harassment to
which they are subject both individually and as a people).
Continued injustice is a festering sore that lends itself to the
rationalization of the feelings of inferiority, humiliation, and
shame, the resulting resentments and hatred, and the desire
for revenge that drive the terrorists – although it is not the
actual reason and cause of Islamic terrorism.

Another aspect of the homework to be done by the West is
for it to reassess its own policies with a view toward making
them less short-sighted and more in keeping with its own
principles of democracy, freedom, human rights. Being inter-

ested only in one's own quick profit or tactical advantage while ignoring the long-range effects and the broader context of one's actions; supporting autocratic or criminal regimes for ideological or economic benefits, as frequently happens, is unacceptable. Especially also the West has to realize that to militarily interfere only briefly in a region, upsetting the traditional local scene, and then leave the region to its fate again ignores its inherent responsibility for the consequences of its interference, above all for doing everything in its power to see to it that the operation might become a lasting success.

As to the second aspect of the Western response to Islamic terrorism (the external response), an idea expressed time and again by many well-meaning people in the West is to engage on a mental and psychological level in an intensified "dialogue of civilizations" and, in practical economic regards, disburse more development aid and insure a fairer distribution of wealth. In itself, dialogue is always something good, and the task of the future will indeed be a "dialogue of civilizations" (between the West and the civilizations of Black Africa, the Islamic countries, the Far East, etc.). But this is a long-range project, and it would be naive to expect that in this way the immediate problem of Islamic terrorism could be answered. In addition, the proposal of a dialogue might in this case even be a mistake since it ignores the fact that the problem behind Islamic terrorism is the objective conflict between two different *historical stages* of cultural development or logical statuses of consciousness. A meaningful dialogue requires that both sides be on the same level, which is not the case here. By advocating such a dialogue, the false impression is created that there were no historical gap between the two civilizations. In addition, terrorism as such precludes dialogue. Just as the terrorists themselves would never be available for a dialogue, so not either the humiliated, shamed soul in the ordinary person in Islamic countries, a soul craving for the restoration of its honor through revenge.

The other suggestion (financial aid, fairer distribution of wealth) also seems to be off the mark in this context. Aid from the Western world would only deepen the feeling of humiliation and shame. Shame does not want help, not betterment, but revenge, death, destruction. The unequal distribution of wealth is not the real problem behind Islamic terrorism. The problem is the historical gap between the objective consciousness inherent in the modern world in which the Moslems, too, are living and the subjective consciousness that they still hold on to. And it is the omitted homework that is actually necessitated by this gap.

Particularly inappropriate is the proposal of some groups in the West that the Western countries apologize to the Third World for the former colonialism. This would only legitimate the inferiority complex and the feeling of victimization.

Another grave mistake, as I see it, is the thrust made by the fifth international conference of the "Forum 2000" in Prague called by Václav Havel, the thrust towards a sacralization of politics in the sense of a "world ethics." According to news reports, Havel is supposed to have demanded a "great spiritual coalition," a "globalization of goodness," because "the time has come for those humans who feel responsible for the future of mankind upon this planet." A combined response to the "globalization of evil," is called for, he said.[9] – This is a wrong move. The proposed "sacralization" walks into the trap of the Islamic terrorists. *They* think in sacral terms ("the Great Devil"). In Islamic countries one of the greatest problems is the tendency towards politicizing religion and a subjecting politics and all social life to (so-called) religion, which in this way becomes totalitarian and an ideology. Under the condi-

---

[9] Karl-Peter Schwarz, "Die Prager Weltethik," in: *FAZ* No. 242, 18 Oct. 2001, p. 16.

tions of modernity, religion is only tolerable if it knows its place: knows itself to have the status of no more than a private hobby. It does not matter so much whether in sacralizing politics one stands up for Good or for Evil; the important thing is that this kind of sacralization is overcome altogether, this mystification through one's inflating concrete human conflicts of interests into a fight between "Good" and "Evil." In accordance with our tradition of the Enlightenment, our thinking and acting has to become more pragmatic, rather than loaded with numinous power words. We don't need a flowery "world ethics"; we do need better international laws as well as institutions for their effective enforcement. The whole ideological, moralistic, numinous superstructure has to be seen through and given up.

As long as there are not sufficient international laws and no effective international law-enforcement agencies, war-like actions will be unavoidable. Here I want to oppose the contempt for violence prevalent in Europe these days. In some cases, violence is the *preferred* reaction. In their thinking, e.g., about the fight against terrorism idealistic pacifists start from on top, from ideas and ideals, from their wishes and hopes. They do not reckon with the immensely real and unwavering existence of the terror movement, rooted as it is down below in the soil of deepest, most passionate emotions. We have to stay faithful to the earth. Better insights, well-meaning intentions, one's good example and friendly complaisance are insufficient. Some conflicts have to be fought through and settled through fighting. Actually existing attitudes that are outdated or false can frequently not simply be overcome through dialogues, instruction and learning from others. They require to be *really* worked off through *real* suffering: one's own experience of their factual failure and the concomitant necessity of an unconditional surrender to the up-to-date status of consciousness. Communism was not overcome through discussions, but through the obvious factual collapse of the Soviet Union just as decades earlier National Socialism was overcome through its total defeat in World War II. One has the learn the hard way, in accordance with the maxim of "Zeus who leads us the way of wisdom": *páthei máthos* ("having learned [or become wise or become conscious] through suffering").[10] Only then has the old attitude indeed (in deed, in fact, in the flesh, objectively) been overcome (and not merely perfunctorily, "theoretically" and subjectively), and has the price of one's liberation from it been fully paid. And the new attitude also has to be acquired the hard way, from scratch and step by step, so as to be rooted in the reality of one's whole being. It cannot be simply imported, such as in school, where to a large degree available knowledge is "imported" by the minds of pupils.

Terrorism as an Integral Part of the Modern World

In conclusion I want to make two brief comments on the "message" that the phenomenon of terrorism at large (not only Islamic terrorism in particular) in the modern world has for us. This phenomenon reveals the *fundamental* vulnerability of the modern world, fundamental because it is a vulnerability from within the system. In this sense terrorism takes its place among a number of phenomena that manifest the present-day status of the constitution of reality. The level of concrete, tangible entities on which formerly the Other used to appear (such as during the time of conventional wars, with two armies openly and above-board vis-à-vis each other) is outdated. Now the "enemy" attacks the system itself insidiously and intangibly from within itself: in the case of individuals through autoimmune diseases, and illnesses like AIDS

---

[10] Aeschylus, *Agamemnon*, line 177.

and cancer; in the information society through computer viruses; politically through terrorism (cf. the so-called "sleepers"!).

One cannot always be on guard and prepared for everything. Just as with unprotected sex, one's careful attention in thousands of instances is not credited against the future; one single minor lack of vigilance can be the loophole through which a catastrophe may slip in. In a world to a large extent governed by the wish to control everything so as to achieve total and guaranteed safety, terrorism reminds us of the vulnerability which is part of and essential to being alive.

The second comment refers to a general character of the age: the lid is off the box; all evil spirits are loose. Modernity means life in a truly *open* society. The money-stage of consciousness with its absolute abstractness, its atomization (individualism) and its "Now!" culture undermined all moral scruples, restraints, bonds, and a feeling of solidarity and responsibility for the common weal. With the end of the cold war, which with its nuclear threat was able to put the lid back on one last time, the last objective restraint was removed. Now human existence has been absolutely released.[11] The unthinkable has become thinkable. Red Cross helpers are no longer safe. No consideration is taken for civilians uninvolved in a conflict, neither by crazed gunmen nor by terrorists. One can no longer count on a natural wish of terrorists to survive. The condition under which nuclear power stations could be considered safe is no longer valid. Small children are being sexually abused and murdered. Biological, chemical, nuclear terror attacks cannot be precluded. The fantasy that we could live in a "Garden of Humane Existence" dissolves. We are again living in the jungle.

---

[11] I am speaking here on a fundamental ontological or logical level, the level of human existence as such, not on the empirical or pragmatic level of individual, personal experience. The majority of individuals (as egos) are still restrained by moral compunctions. But not so the soul of man.

Wolfgang Giegerich is a Jungian analyst in private practice in Wörthsee near Munich, Germany, and author of many books; his articles have frequently appeared in *Spring Journal* and in the *Eranos Yearbooks*.

The Motivation of Terrorists

Adolf Guggenbühl-Craig

Terrorist actions appear to contradict our knowledge of human psychology. As a rule we human beings have the desire to live and are afraid to die. But this does not seem to be the case with terrorists. Not only are they ready to destroy and kill, but they are prepared to die, too, to sacrifice themselves. With the intention of killing others, they blow themselves up as well.

Where some religious fundamentalists are concerned, "suicide bombing" is a "rational" decision. To die in a holy war, to die in the service of a god might guarantee immediate entrance into paradise. The rewards of holy war are not new: In many of the crusades the warriors were forgiven their sins at the beginning of the battle – they were "saved." Many fundamentalist Muslims believe that fighting for Allah guarantees them a place in paradise. Based on these promises, it seems to be quite a reasonable decision to die in the service of God, of Allah, etc.

But the promise of "instant paradise" is not valid for all terrorists: Some are not religious fundamentalists. Furthermore, if a terrorist has the slightest feeling for other human beings, killing hundreds or thousands of people might be too high a price to pay for paradise.

Depth psychology shows us some deeper motivation for the deeds of terrorists who kill themselves to kill others.

Freud wrote a booklet called: *Beyond the Pleasure Principle*.[1] In it he postulated that there are two basic instincts in human beings: Thanatos and Eros, the death instinct and the love for life. The love for life is easy to understand and quite acceptable. But what about this strange death instinct? The death instinct implies that we have a drive and a longing for death, for our own death and for the death of others. The idea of the death instinct apparently comes from Sabina Spielrein, a former patient of C.G. Jung. Freud seems to have taken up the idea under the influence of the first World War when millions of young men willingly sacrificed themselves and killed millions of the enemy. Human beings, "beyond the pleasure principle," seem to be continually torn between Eros and Thanatos.

The idea of a death instinct was rejected by most Freudians. It seemed to be completely against the laws of nature, against the only two laws governing all biological life: survive and reproduce.

Oddly enough, Jung presented an idea similar to the death instinct. He said that the core of our shadow – the archetypal center – is the suicidal maniac and murderer.

So both these founding fathers of modern, depth psychology suspect that death has as much an attraction for human beings as has life. The history of humankind certainly shows that these ideas are not completely wrong. For as long as recorded human history, we have observed the phenomenon that men – and at times women too – are ready to sacrifice themselves with enthusiasm or to indulge in massacres. *Dulce est pro patria mori*. At the beginning of the first World War thousands of young Europeans marched enthusiastically into the deadliest battles. Thousands of young men volunteered

[1] Freud, S., *Standard Edition* 18, 1920.

during the Second World War in Japan to be Kamikaze pilots. It is not possible to describe or mention all the examples where and when human beings sacrificed themselves gladly or committed massacres – there are too many, the most recent being Rwanda, Cambodia, Stalin's Russia, Nazi Germany, etc., etc.

Phenomenologically, it is difficult not to see that self-destruction and the murder of others seems to have a very strong appeal under certain circumstances. But luckily, in the tension between Thanatos and Eros, it is usually Eros which dominates. The tension between these polarities of life and death, however, is never easy to bear.

Terrorism is a unique solution to the conflict between Thanatos and Eros. In the name of Eros, in the name of some noble cause, one can kill and destroy others and oneself. When roles were reversed in the history of Christian-Muslim relations, Christian crusaders could live out their death instinct by murdering thousands of Muslims (and Jews), and they could live out their suicidal urges by sacrificing themselves for the conquest of the holy land. Today, Islamic terrorists can act as suicide bombers to destroy civilians and soldiers, and they attain the status of martyrs for their god. Apparently, "noble goals" make it possible to unite the death instinct with Eros. The impossible tension between Thanatos and Eros is resolved in an explosive, ecstatic moment.

The Christian and Muslim religions of today recognize indirectly the death instinct: In the Ten Commandments it says, "Thou shall not kill." To forbid something means that the impulse or action must be tempting. There is no need to forbid something which no one has the desire to do. The Christian religion expressly says: Do not live out the death instinct. And it says too: Try to live out Eros, to "love thy neighbor as thyself." The Ten Commandments would have us tolerate and hold the tension between Thanatos and Eros. Thanatos, however, extends beyond homicidal drives. Freud's hypothesis of the death instinct reminds us that we not only have urges to kill but also to die. Similarly, Jung's hypothesis of the archetypal shadow recognizes murderous and suicidal desires. Psychoanalytic explorations, therefore, can help us to understand the full spectrum of terrorist violence toward self and others.

My reflections show that the motives for terrorism are a fusion between Eros and Thanatos. And my reflections show that terrorists are human beings like ourselves, that they have basically the same kind of psychological problems and are governed by the same archetypes as we are, in this case by the polar archetypes of Eros and Thanatos.

The human psyche is extremely complex. Our intellectual instruments are not really able to deal adequately with the human psyche. Our attempts to deal intellectually with the psyche are only possible by making simplifications. The hypothesis that the two deepest instincts in us are the death instinct and the life instinct, Thanatos and Eros, are obviously simplifications.

Thanatos and Eros are concepts, are words, perhaps images. One word is used to name something extremely complicated. Psychology is only at the beginning and tries with very primitive categories, which are expressed by words, to describe the human psyche. And only when with time psychology becomes less primitive shall we be able to draw the necessary conclusions and to deal more successfully with the phenomenon of terrorism, which is really a psychological phenomenon.

Unlike the study of other archetypes, the study of Eros and Thanatos will probably always present us with no indications. It will present us with mystery – not because we have missed the point because something went wrong in our study, but because we have reached the heart of the matter: Eros and

Thanatos are mysteries. We can understand terrorists from a political point of view. From a psychological perspective the core of their motivation will remain a mystery to us, and perhaps even to themselves. By keeping terrorism within the human circle – a function of Eros – we will at least maintain the potential for dialogue.

I do not know how to use my reflections in dealing concretely and practically in relation to terrorism. However, as an analyst I trust that any increase in human understanding helps us to tolerate and hold the tremendous tensions of our time.

Adolf Guggenbühl-Craig is a psychiatrist in Zurich and a past president of the C.G. Jung Institute there and of the IAAP. His numerous publications include: *Power in the Helping Professions* and *Marriage: Dead or Alive* (both Spring Publications, Woodstock).

The Terror and The Temple

Victor-Pierre Stirnimann

To think is to forget differences.

Jorge Luis Borges

All the people like us are We, and everyone else is
They.

Rudyard Kipling

To be confused about what is different and what is
not, is to be confused about everything.

David Bohm

There are so many worlds, and I have not yet
conquered even one.

Plutarch

The times following a catastrophe are marked by excess.
There is too much information and the emotions have yet to
find their proper place. It may be too soon for us to expect a
transforming reflection about several of the issues at hand:
the many fundamentalisms – where all are soldiers and the
frontiers are internal – the religious differences, and the
ignorance. And still there might be a contribution to be made,
as far as this new kind of terrorism is concerned. A terrorism
that many have called *symbolic*.

Buddhas

Let us start out with a direct statement: the destruction of the two Buddha statues in Afghanistan, in March 2001, points to a parallel with the Twin Towers attacks six months later. It is a parallel that sounds impertinent: if it weren't for the imagistic component and the shallow analogy it suggests, what else would there be in common between the events? Their scale, their consequences, and their culprits were not the same. But there is a lost thread to be found, perhaps, if we probe a bit deeper into the historical antecedents of those statues.

The region which today corresponds to Afghanistan and the Valley of Kashmir used to be a center for the Sarvastivadin school of Buddhism, and there the first Buddha statues were made. For centuries, the religious tradition did not use to represent the Buddha in human form; he and his teachings were rendered only in an allegorical or abstract way. All this was to change, however, around the 4th century B.C., when the region was invaded by Alexander the Great. The Sarvastivadin school (the name meaning literally "everything-exists") absorbed the Greek influence, resulting in the Hellenic representation of Buddha – human-like sculptures, proportionate and serene. It was the birth of the Gandharan style, and similar images quickly spread throughout Asia.

In fact, the Greek influence at the birth of those statues consisted of something much more subtle than human traits carved on a rock. What the Greek invaders brought along with them was the whole destiny behind the word *kolossós*. Before acquiring the late meaning of *big statue*, the *kolossoí* were small puppets made of wood or clay, created to serve as ritual representations of the dead or absent ones – not as imitations, but as *substitutes*.[1] That is why it is not important to consider that no one knew the real face of Buddha, in the 4th century

B.C.: those statues were meant to generate *presence,* to be an opening where the invisible manifests itself. In short: to symbolize.

This way, the Buddha statues were quite important in terms of cultural history: they were a product of the first contacts between two civilizations, the East and the West. Conceived under the tolerant spirit that "everything-exists," they survived until the coming to our times and to the Taliban law – when they suddenly became an offence to the Islamic fundamentalism.

Idolatry is forbidden in Islam, but there was probably more in this iconoclastic drive than first met the eye. The statues had not been worshipped for centuries, and thus represented no threat; in fact, they were little more than remains from a forgotten past. Moreover: if radicalism and religiosity were the only reasons for blowing them up, why turn their destruction into a world press event? *They were only stones*, as the mullah has allegedly said. But the mullah also said, when Western institutions offered to buy the statues: *we prefer to be remembered as the destroyers of statues, rather than as the sellers of them.*

No, there was here a stronger logic in operation, destroyers as opposed to sellers – it is quite likely that the Buddhas turned into a real issue at a very specific moment, when the Taliban leaders were able to realize the statues' importance in view of the Western mentality. By preferring to destroy them, instead of taking advantage of the hegemonic rules of commerce and interchange, they wanted to make a statement. They wanted to carry out a symbolic act, and they aimed it at a public. We may have seen it as an act of cultural self-destruction. It was also an act of terrorism against the West, against something deeply symbolic to their adversaries.

---

[1] Cf. Ginzburg, C., *Wooden Eyes: Nine Reflections on Distance* (M. Ryle & K. Soper, Trans), Columbia University Press, 2001

For the West keeps on building museums and consuming spiritual goods, as if we could pull them out from their time and place – as if we preferred them to be distant from their historical context. It was in the eyes of the Taliban, on the contrary, that the two high Buddhas hardly deserved any attention; they could remain forgotten as mere stone, since the old Buddhist cult that generated them was already dead. No, this was a terrorist attack, perpetrated through the public immolation of a symbolic body.

Here we have a first paradox: in spite of all our media technology, it was through the destruction of the WTC, only six months later, that we learned again what "real time" and "live news" actually mean. By destroying pillars and icons of a still effective world order, the suicidal terrorists created an event that pierced the network of our indifference, and History seemed to wake up from its torpor. As for us, we realize again that historical significance postulates itself, thanks to its raw impact.

It would be useful at this point to retrieve the insightful remarks taken from an Uzbek military newspaper, the *Vatanparvar*, on March 3, 2001 – some days before the explosion of the Buddhas. The author, A. Karimov, denounced the Taliban's intention of exploiting what he defined as a weakness of the Western countries, our willingness to preserve historical and cultural heritages. Then he added that another idea had come to his mind: "what have people not done in the world in order to gain fame, and to ensure that their deeds left an indelible trace in the pages of history? One of them was Herostratus. In order to insure his immortal fame, he chose the simplest and vilest way: he burned down the great temple of Diana in Ephesus. Thinking about it, we may believe that the Taliban have chosen Herostratus's way. ..."

Herostratus, indeed. Could he be a clue, a pre-figuration to lead our way to a deeper understanding of it all?

Herostratus

The Artemision in Ephesus, a temple magnificent enough to be listed among the seven Ancient Wonders of the World, burned down on the night of 21 July 356 B.C. A man called Herostratus had deliberately set the fire, and was later executed for his sacrilege. Before his execution, however, he explained his motives.

Knowing himself as totally devoid of any trait of excellence, Herostratus tried to immortalize his name through the only other way he could find – destroying something immortal, in order to participate in the immortality of what he had destroyed. The Ephesians still tried to expurgate his name from all historical records – but Herostratus won, making himself immortal through the unconceivable nature of his crime.

Herostratus's question can be expressed as follows: how do you make yourself meaningful, significant in your individual existence, when you do not possess anything of recognizable value to your own time and culture? And the answer he presented could not be more radical: you can overcome your mediocrity, if only you sacrifice yourself together with a valuable offering to the Gods of your era. To destroy, but as a means to possess. Yet this individual went even further: he destroyed/possessed what was arguably the most sacred and valued place of the world he knew. By committing this unthinkable transgression, while looking forward to its certain punishment, his terrorism put him by force in the center of his own cosmos.

Herostratus takes to the extreme his protest against the predicament that an unequal destiny (his insignificance as an individual) imposes upon the equality of desire (his longing for recognition). In so doing, he reveals what happens to the human need for self-expression, once it is distorted by an excessively abstract and universal perspective: it becomes a quest for fame, a craving for approved predicates. That's the root of all predicaments, by the way: a predicate.

Herostratus offers an evocation or model allowing us to better figure the power of a suicide, when it is associated to a symbolic destruction of collective magnitude. Would it be possible, through his story, to reinforce our first analogy, which seeks to associate the Buddhas' explosion to the September attacks? To begin with, it makes us recall how much these events rely on a fundamental principle of terrorism, its intimate relationship with publicity. We cannot fully understand the destruction of the Buddhas without the notion that we ourselves be placed before the stage as an audience; and the choice of the American targets cannot be explained without referral to their public exposure, their notoriety and world significance. In both cases, destruction was perpetrated in order *to be seen*. (As Herostratus's plan relied on that he was sure to be discovered.)

This is, however, only the more trivial aspect of the analogy. It is the iconoclastic component that should be stressed here, the particularly religious status of what was to be destroyed. On this account, the deepest target of the aggression consisted of the very beliefs that sustain our everyday life. Let's take the first iconoclastic act: at the end it was not an aggression against the old Sarvastivadin school of Buddhism (if "everything-exists," there would also be a time and place for the armed fundamentalist ...), but mainly against our tolerant consumerism of all images, our passion for signs to be infinitely interchanged. When they decided that the statues had no exchange value, but only value as something-to-be-destroyed, it was the meaning of our own rituals to suffer the attack. And all this, of course, only by way of rehearsal. Then there was the great strike against one of our temples, the

World *Trade* Center and the architectural wonder of its high columns touching the sky.

It is true that there were other targets and victims on September 11; but our collective imagination is prone to omit them, dazzled by the image of the towers imploding, and also because the South of Manhattan is the real center of our world's capital.

We watched, in "real time," the equivalent to what must have been, in 356 B.C., the fire at the Artemision. And at this point we should widen the range of our reflection, drifting away from the present events and towards Artemis – yes, we'll have to deal with mythology – for she must have been the main offended party, according to the story.

Artemis

Artemis, along with Gorgon and Dionysus, pointed to the alien and the different.[2] All three regulated the contact between here and beyond, between the limits and their absence, each one representing a specific threat to an established order. Artemis ruled over the boundary between the civilized and the savage, the space between the city and the forest; in human existence, her special moment was the *parthenia*: a stage at which the Greek young girls had already left infancy, around nine years of age, but were not yet ready for marriage. Puberty, adolescence, when one is no longer nature/infancy, but is not civilization yet and does not take an active part in the *polis*.

Artemis restrained transgressions, the autonomy of every natural impulse opposing itself to a new order. She could also appear in the battlefield, when the conflicts were about to

---

[2] Cf. Vernant, J.-P., *La mort dans les yeux. Figures de l'Autre en Grèce ancienne*, Hachette, Paris, 1985

become barbaric. Her weapons were the disguise of the footprints, the bold tactics, the infiltration, and the blow which bewildered the enemies.

Another peculiarity of Artemis: her rituals were practiced with the use of masks. The divinities of transition and otherness demanded masks because the realms they defined were mutually incommensurate; no adequate translation could trespass their borders, and thus *one side could never reveal its own face to the other*. The mask was the intermediary link, as it were, the transitional identity which enabled an anticipation of what was yet to be.

Let us return to our thread: if we were to build a temple for this goddess, would there be a better place than Ephesus, at the entrance door of Asia Minor, at the transitional zone between the Greek world and its otherness, between the West and the East? And as for Herostratus – was he not an exact personification of the autonomy which infiltrates the night and reacts against the established order? Herostratus's defiance was the reaction of someone who recognized himself as insignificant according to the rules of the game, and found only one way to force the recognition of his own face, his difference – through barbarism. And what is left of him, after more than two thousand years, is only the mask of a name – perhaps not even his real name – one last trace of a terrorist's *persona*.

But these associations lead us to an intriguing result: we should ask the goddess herself about the source of the impulse which put her temple in flames. For it is an imbalance on her own sphere of influence that might explain Herostratus's excess. This way, Artemis was not only the target of the sacrilege, but a more active part in our plot – perhaps, who knows, even its own protagonist. After all, the story does not close where we stopped examining it.

Plutarch wrote that the goddess was unable to defend her temple that night, because she was very busy, supervising a special birth. For while the Artemision was burning away, as the Greek historians used to tell, a woman was giving birth to Alexander the Great.

Alexander

In the legends, at least, there is no space for coincidences. Alexander, the ideal pre-figuration of a great biography, could not be more different from Herostratus. Born to make history, Aristotle's private pupil, we all learned at school how the Macedonian expanded the Hellenic world through military campaigns taking him to the extremes of Asia, up to what we know today as Afghanistan, Pakistan and India. In fact, his imperial expansion was the factor responsible for the meeting of cultures that produced our Buddha statues. (Incidentally, the contact between the peoples happened to be fruitful in both ways: the legend tells us that in Balkh, approximately where today is Mazar-i-Sharif, in northern Afghanistan, Alexander met the beautiful princess who became his only wife and mother of his only son – *Roxanne*.) Even in our days some ethnologists still believe in the hypothesis/fantasy of the possible "Greeks" of Afghanistan, descendants of Alexander's troops. These would be the Kalash or Kafir peoples, dwelling on the mountains on the northeast of the country. What used to be called Kafiristan inspired Rudyard Kipling in his famous short story, "The Man Who Would be King," a short fable about imperialism and narcissism. ...

There are controversies as far as Alexander's military genius is concerned. But there are no doubts about what he accomplished in just a few years. Alexander's campaigns opened what was then the known world to an incalculable economic and commercial development, creating in their track the routes of interchange between East and West, and making lucrative enterprises sprawl everywhere. The circulation of large amounts of gold financed all this expansion, because Alexander forced the Persian dynasty to open its treasuries. With all that, Hellenism can be considered the first worldwide economic boom. The world trade system developed at the time remained practically untouched for more than two thousand years, until the industrial revolution. In other words: Alexander the Great personifies the first large *globalization* movement.

Barbarism

Having Aristotle as his preceptor, Alexander descends directly from the lineage of spirits who founded our Western thought: Socrates was Plato's teacher, who taught Aristotle, who educated Alexander in philosophy, ethics, politics, and medicine. In a certain way, Alexander represents the first totally pragmatic manifestation of the Western *logos* which had just been born. And Alexander's practical vision was to become, in the end, a main cause of disagreement with his master. A disagreement which changed History: Aristotle was of the opinion that non-Greek peoples were nothing but savages, barbarians, and therefore should be disregarded; Alexander, on the contrary, radicalized what was already implicit in the very origin of the terms: if "barbarian" is he whose speech we do not understand (speaks bar-bar), he who does not speak Greek, then the key would be in hellenization; the foreigners, once assimilated into Greek culture, would stop being barbaric. Therefore, Alexander's empire could expand itself to all the confines of the world, *provided that it was built upon an universalization of the language.*

This reasoning is clearly behind what was the cleverest tactical maneuver of the Macedonian: to stimulate his soldiers to get married in conquered lands, creating blood ties between the foreigners and the Greeks. This way, the military superiority represented only the first moment of the Alexandrian strategy of conquest; the second would be the strengthening of the commercial ties, and the third, decisive, the cultural unification.

Seen from this angle, Alexander's history unfolds from a traditional core of polarities, the one opposing center and periphery, the civilized and the savage, "We" and the "Others." The very polarities that articulate the problem of otherness. Yes, Artemis once more. Alexander turned his life into an attempt to respond to this problem, to the challenge of the distance, the difference, the intelligibility of the other. With the military expeditions he would surpass the distances, with the commerce – equalization of desires – he would make the differences irrelevant, and with the cutting power of the Greek *logos* he would untie all the knots of intelligibility.

The famous story of the Gordian knot is a good illustration of how aggressive and hasty that strategy was. In what was then the capital of ancient Phrygia, the oracles had determined that the first person to ride up to the temple of Zeus in a wagon was to be chosen as the next king. Gordius innocently fulfilled the oracle and gained the throne. One of his first acts was to dedicate his wagon to Zeus and to place it near the temple, the yoke tied to the pole by a very intricate knot of cornel bark. Then, the oracle disclosed another prophecy: anyone who succeeded in untying the knot would be the conqueror of all Asia. According to the story, Alexander came and got over this obstacle by taking a very characteristic approach – instead of untying the knot, he drew his sword and cut it.

The fantasy which possessed Alexander was to transform the world in a mirror. Freed from the intricacies of a decoding effort, from the Gordian Knot of interpretation, differences annulled or turned into indifferences, his goal was to create an uniform reality, so uniform that it could reflect back to him his own vision. Thus he would be able to gaze into what he really wanted to know: himself. Alexander died young, however, and did not see the completion of his project, did not conquer the whole of Asia. He didn't *untie* the knot, after all.

Nietzsche

There is a downside to everything, and this also applies to Alexander's globalization. Nietzsche identified it, completely active, in the Germany of his own time. He named "Alexandrian" what in his diagnosis would be the noblest form of Greek optimism, the theoretical one: "It believes that it can correct the world by knowledge, guide life by science, and actually *confine the individual within a limited sphere of solvable problems*, from which he can cheerfully say to life: 'I desire you; you are worth knowing.' "[3]

According to Nietzsche, the whole modern world was entangled in the web of Alexandrian culture. A culture that required – to use Nietzsche's terms – some sort of "slave class" to subsist and yet lived in optimistic denial of such need, proclaiming the "dignity of man": a contradiction that would end up leading to "dreadful destruction."

It is important, at this point, to recall that the world today is a very different place from what Germany used to be in the middle of the industrial revolution. Yet the issue is unavoidable: have we really become *less* Alexandrian? The answer

[3] Nietzsche, F., "The Birth of Tragedy" (W. Kaufmann, Trans.), in *Basic Writings of Nietzsche*, Random House, New York, 1968, p. 109. Italics mine.

should bring us back to the urgency of our times; but first we need to tie together the loose ends of this mysterious connection between Herostratus and Alexander.

Knot

Plutarch tells us that Alexander cried while hearing Anaxarcus's speech about the infinite number of worlds in the universe – for he had not totally conquered his own yet. The Macedonian's desire for conquest was insatiable – his expansion movement receding only when his army refused to go any farther, and Alexander becoming ill shortly thereafter – and the same could be said of his craving for fame. This is very well illustrated in an episode that may tighten our intricate knot, the one which ties Alexander's destiny to a certain temple and its arsonist. In 333 B.C., the Macedonian emperor was in Ephesus, and there he saw the Artemision still being rebuilt. It is said that he offered to finance the completion of the works, *provided that he received all the credit for it and his name were carved on the temple.* The city administrators, however, managed to avoid his ambiguous generosity with a reply full of psychological subtlety: *it is not fitting that one god should build a temple for another god.*

Herostratus burned the temple while driven by a quest for immortality, and Alexander tried to finance its reconstruction exactly for the same motive. The same need to leave behind a mark, creating or destroying: perhaps Herostratus and Alexander should be understood as two faces of a single theme, with their aggressive response to the state of things, their cult to their own personality, their potential for violence. A centrifugal face and another centripetal: the one seeks to expand the world while the other tries to get hold of its symbolical center.

This alternative is always there, especially during adolescence, when we need to metabolize the pressure to enter the adults' game, the violence of the norms over the still untamed parts of our nature. The response can be Alexandrian and self-confident, the "get out there and conquer it"; or it can be the reflux of depredation and delinquency, the transgressor Herostratus smashing shop windows during the early hours of the morning. In both movements, however, something always ends up being sacrificed: there is neither recognition nor assimilation of that inarticulate kernel of sense which is felt to pertain to each individuality. That is the reason behind the identical thirst for notoriety – it can offer some relief for what is lacking. In the case of our transgressor, this is quite clear: what justifies his terrorist modality of destruction is that it must be noticed. If I don't deserve recognition, then let me be identified through the damage I create.

And what about our conqueror's case? It is Nietzsche who gave us the key, when he said that the Alexandrian mentality confines the individual to the sphere of problems that its own categories can solve. For the sake of efficacy, all differences should disappear in the sharing of the same set of values and attributes, and therefore the only possible compensation for what has been lost will be the exceptional outcome, the extraordinary success.

Herostratus already denounced that this was the topic in question, when he justified himself by saying that he did not possess any attribute or quality which would make him famous. Herostratus is the plebeian, anonymous version of the same Alexandrian man, the man in the historical moment when his nature starts to submit itself to Aristotelian normalization, the moment when, properly speaking, the Western vision of the world is about to be born. Herostratus feels himself excluded from it; Alexander takes it as the foundation for an empire. In short, it may be said that our reflections end up acquiring a philosophical flavor. For what unites and opposes our two figures is the expansion of the Western *logos* and its way to deal with differences. To put in another way: when Alexander decides to cut off the Gordian knot, instead of untying it, what is lost?

Singularity

What is lost, above all, is a space for the mystery of everything that cannot be said.

First, the attention for the enigma of the *Other*. The West begins with the principle that only what is thought can exist, and that thought exists only when it can be put into language. The perspective of the Other, he who does not share our language, cannot be thought, does not exist. Our option is then either to ignore/deny, or to translate/betray in our own terms. Herostratus follows the way of negation, Alexander the way of betrayal.

Second, what is lost has already been anticipated above: a look upon the miracle of *singularity*. Every language is constituted of universals, our words are generalities – and yet nothing, absolutely nothing of our experience is identical to any other thing. (Have we said that all words are generalities? All of them, except the proper names. This way we clarify our two characters' obsession for the immortality of their own names. Celebrity is the only compensation for our blindness to the singular.) Each individual is unrepeatable, and each moment, each small particle of living experience cannot be transmitted, communicated, in what makes it really unique. It can not even be *thought*; for our thinking depends on labels, concepts, and formulae which separate for us the relevant from the irrelevant. But there are some epiphanic moments, when our awareness has a glimpse at things, either because they shout at us or because we find a way to *look* at them. And then, in no time at all, we visit the reverse of things. Perhaps singularity will never be turned into *knowledge*, but it still continues to persist as *information*.[4]

Now we should stop these musings and return to the concreteness of our contemporary war, with its peculiar horrors and uncertainties. Because if there is anything new in sight, it is that the individual has been introduced in the scenario.

War

Under many aspects, this is a war like the previous ones. But an important difference lies on the fact that one of the antagonists is called, simply, "the terrorism." What we have now is a war where only one of the sides has a regular army, the remains of a common identity. What this army proposes to face is a more or less abstract mob, without shape and without center, where, at times, the functional connection between its members fades into disappearance. When the Anthrax envelopes first came to the scene, for instance – where did the attacks come from? Opportunistic alliances between foreign and local terrorism challenge all logic of state. In this war, the non-cohesion brings the individual factor to the foreground, liberating it for a new scale of intervention; now, the individual can be the army itself.

Suicidal terrorism and isolated attacks always existed, to make up for the weakness or defeat of a military power. This

[4] These critical remarks about the limits of the West are certainly not new; behind them are the echoing voices of a precise lineage of thought: Nietzsche, Heidegger, Deleuze ... but it would be only fair to remember how much this theme could be profoundly Jungian, too. For what we should point as the characteristically Jungian question is: how can the individual, the unique, recognize himself and find expression beyond (or beneath) the universal dynamics of instincts, images and ideas?

time, however, the scenario is different, as we are dealing here with a conflict which could not become the confrontation of two regular armies. Formally, this is a conflict between Herostratus and Alexander.

It is time to face what appears to be a problem of this parallel, the fact that Herostratus sought recognition, while the current terrorist seems not to mind his remaining anonymous. Let's see through it: the suicidal martyr becomes a hero before his people; the paranoid sending white powder through the post perpetuates himself by spreading his personal beliefs – all these violent acts have a symbolic component, and all of them are in the pursuit of some sort of abstract immortality. No, Herostratus was also anonymous when he set fire to the temple, his anonymity was a pre-condition for the motive and means of his crime, as it is in anonymity that we find the strategic core of our present war. And Herostratus's symbolic crime was also aimed at the universal.

This is, in many senses, a conflict between the singularity and the universal, having the symbolic as the battlefield. In our memory of September 11, the indignation stems from the deaths and the suffering; but the terror comes from the image.

September

The attacks on September 11 would not be feasible in a world where the Alexandrian impulse had not got close to its extreme. Technological knowledge has shortened/civilized all distances to the same extent that it has exposed our own precariousness. In the months that followed, there was an attempt to give a very specific face to the antagonists. At the same time, the discourse regressed to archaic language forms, to the sheer abstraction of the "Good *versus* Evil." Such symptoms of weak articulation should not divert us from our focus: on that day a group of anonymous individuals, disposing of little more than cunning and resolve, altered the course of things and put to their service the big escalade of destruction. The authorities insisted: they were trained, sponsored, supported by a huge underground network. It could be. And yet the image of the underground network, without much identity and dimension, offers the exact measure of what really happened: anyone, in principle, could have taken part in it; *anyone could have contributed to change History*. For the criminals who changed our future did not need much technology, and did not need a lot of money. This is the greatest subversion, what every government must try to conceal: that the real weapons were patience, which provided for a long preparation, and determination, which ensured the suicidal component of the attacks.

Paul Virilio has been saying that every technology also brings with it its own new accident modality. Well, this is a war of accidents, and in this sense it can mark the end of the post-Hiroshima era. Power and destruction are no longer the prerogative of a select club. In principle, at least, anyone is able to hijack a plane, to start a shooting in schools or government centers, to become a terrorist. The Evil requires no face, and this gives back to the individual, in an apparent paradox, the responsibility for the course of things. The place for the alienated victim, the passive spectator gradually fades away. There is no distance any longer, and every hierarchy offers only an illusion of security. Every individual is a Herostratus, a micro-controller of things, even if just for the reason that he can decide *not* to participate in some destruction, *not* to hijack something and throw it against some building.

This is a very difficult message from September: power starts to decentralize, and the Artemis issue, the opposition between the center and the periphery, becomes increasingly meaningless on this climax of Alexandrian civilization: nations do not follow their own paths anymore, whereas singularity, the accident, is emerging from all corners, faceless, non-Aristotelian, imploding essences without our being able to put it into thought. Not exactly the stuff empires are built upon.

Gog and Magog

We should not concentrate too much on the attacks. Herostratus is not to be restricted to Islamic fundamentalists; he could easily be seen as a typically American phenomenon, like the teenager who initiates a shooting at his own school. We can find his traces in Oklahoma City, or in the middle-aged citizen who massacred politicians at the House of Representatives in Zug, Switzerland, or in any young and uneducated individual from a Third World country who sees in a gun his only gateway to achievement. All willing to touch History, all dying for immortality.

Accordingly, the Islamic culture is also, in its origin, quite Alexandrian. Alexander is mentioned in the Koran, exalted as a civilizing hero who rescues the backward peoples of a distant land (the land of the two mountains), using the power of his technique (the construction of an iron wall) in order to protect them from Gog and Magog, the chaos and destruction forces. No, this plot suits both sides; it is the same dilemma posed by the reality of the Other and his perceived barbarism. Perhaps the two cultures in question are not different *enough*, and this could help to explain their rivalry.

Clearing

There is no balance in the relationship between *polis* and forest, civilization and barbarism, center and periphery; these opposites do not work any longer. But then what is lost is the intermediate space defined by their tension, the dwelling place for that principle which the Greeks called Artemis. Heidegger, in his late years, used to be fascinated by an image: *die Lichtung,* the clearing. A reasonably unobstructed space in the forest, or perhaps the surroundings of the *polis* – for the city is always *surrounded* by a forest, no matter if concrete, logical or metaphorical – where former oppositions could try to meet and make a different sort of contact. This is what we lack the most: clearings, appearing and disappearing, teaching us about this deep truth of our human history, that civilizations are nothing but camping sites. This was Artemis's terrain and she was the protagonist of a story identifying our theme – to remind us that the future (not only the past) is always wild, too, and that our reflection cannot anticipate it.

Yes: we need a *logos* of the difference, a "deconstruction," but we need more than intellectual critique. For many years, the call has been for another way of thinking, another myth, a new sense of time. And this is not obtained on order, nor can it be instituted through reflection. It depends on the workings of the objective psyche (which is a fancy way to refer to the unknown), even if it is brought forward, here and there, through the initiatives of some first individuals. Maybe this is what our many disciples of Herostratus come to show. That Artemis, the obsolete, still demands reparation.

Alexandria

We did not mention the psychopathy, or the criminal element. We focused upon cultures and anonymous individuals. The progress of our narrative, however, relates the war between cultures (and its associated theme, the globalization) to a new form of terrorism (and its associated theme, the singularity). This association belongs already to collective consciousness, but the story expressing it may give us many other clues concerning much that still remains in the shade.

It is said that the foundation ritual of Alexandria (the most important city built by Alexander, a city about to reopen its great temple, the library) was accompanied by a strong omen. Alexander had ordered to plot the perimeter of the city. His men took meal and outlined the area; and then birds of various species picked up the meal and flew off in all directions. Curious to know the meaning of this event, Alexander consulted his soothsayers. They said to him: *this city which has been built shall feed the entire world; and the men born in it shall be everywhere; like birds, they shall travel through the entire world.*

This would be the most luminous promise of the Alexandrian world; if the augurs could speak frankly, however, perhaps they would have said that *the food, the resources, are dispersed and consumed without any distribution control; in the process all limits are lost, along with everything that can define the future city, the civilization.*

Roxanne

What happened to her, the Afghan princess who offered herself in marriage to Alexander? Roxanne was the only woman of the most powerful man on earth, and she gave him a son. It seems that, exhausting himself with his conquests and dying young, Alexander did not know how to protect his wife and his heir. Roxanne had to flee, carrying her son, from the generals who intended to share between them the enormous empire. The generals eventually found her, and Roxanne was killed, together with the child who was to inherit the world.

We belong to an old tradition which symbolically associates the feminine to the soul and the challenge of relating to the Other, and legends do not care for accidents. Alexander's wife, murdered, is a perfect image for all the soul which is lost at each historical cycle of global expansion.[5]

Iris

Is it too outdated, to be open for meaningful coincidences? While these pages are written, the *National Geographic Magazine* announces that they have found again the Afghan girl whose picture was put on their cover in 1985 – a picture that remains as one of the strongest images in the last decades. Her name is Sharbat Gula, and she would be, at the time, less than thirteen.

Nothing replaces the presence of the image, but we could say that the impact caused by the girl comes from her eyes. Their beauty do not seem entirely human: her look is a bit wild, as if it had just come out of the forest, unique and absolute. They say that the patterns of the human iris are still more unmistakable than fingerprints. And it was through this way that they found her again, precociously old and almost unrecognizable after many years of chaos and destruction, lost among millions of other refugees from History, millions

---

[5] Perhaps we are only left to sing the fate of another Roxanne, the prostitute from the popular song: *Roxanne, you don't have to put on the red light...*

of other people with absolutely no significance: through her eyes. Eyes such as those do not repeat themselves, glaring in their sheer singularity. And yet their wild shine – in the girl of the right age – seems to warn: if Artemis would take a human shape, this would be her look.

This is the short-circuit mentioned by C.G.Jung, the cognitive/experiential wonder which our theory has not yet been able to entirely absorb. For it is the understanding *and* its reverse, it is the singular *and* the universal, it is the irreplaceable *and* the eternal, a particle-and-wave paradox in the microphysics of our sight. Her name is Sharbat Gula, but we could just as well call her Roxanne.

Yes: a symbol, maybe. We have spoken so much lately about the imaginal reality. One should also speak about the reality which summons us from this image, ageless as the world, a portrait of all our marginality and exclusion.

Victor-Pierre Stirnimann received a diploma in analytical psychology from the C.G. Jung Institute, Zurich, and and a philosophy degree from the Universidade de São Paulo. A former consultant in the area of corporate education, he has lectured and published on philosophy and psychology in his native Brazil. He is now in private practice in São Paulo.

A Safe Place

Verena Kast

The Need for a Safe Place

If a traumatic event like September 11 occurs, there is not only anxiety, anger and a questioning of why it could have happened, who is to blame for it, the grieving, the loss of confidence in life in general: people also want to learn something from this crucial experience. If something can be learned which helps us to go on with life in a confident way – even with the danger of terrorism – the human catastrophe would not be completely absurd.

We feel more Threatened than ever Before

Did the whole world really change on September 11? This is a statement born out of the shock in the face of the utmost brutality of the terrorist act. But terrorism has existed for many years. Suicidal assassins have existed since the war in Lebanon in the Eighties; it is a method of engagement much more dangerous than bombs. And it provokes the question of why people decide to sacrifice their lives in this way. Of course, there may be religious convictions, but there could also be psycho-social reasons: if you don't feel respected, if you have no future, if you are not of any value to the social group to which you belong, then you have great potential value as a living bomb – and you obtain an identity in dying which is communicated to the whole world and produces horror.

The world changed on September 11 in that we are no longer able to hide some deep problems between different nations. I do not think the world has become a more dangerous place than it had been before. But perhaps we feel more threatened than before and we have to deal with this.

The Search for a Safe Place

If something terrible happens which makes people feel deeply uncertain, then human beings look for a safe place. In my opinion, this is the most important task which has to be undertaken – by each individual and in groups to which one belongs – now and in the future.

What does this mean: a safe place? It is a space where you feel safe in an unsafe world. If a statesman after a cruel assassin on politicians openly declines a bodyguard and the use of a private car in favor of public transportation, he communicates, without verbalizing it, a feeling of being safe in spite of the danger, and also declares an unwillingness to share the panic of some people, by not being in panic. That does not mean not being concerned, not being determined to face the problem and to find solutions, but it means preserving the feeling of being safe in a unsafe world. Feeling safe helps by reacting not with uncontrolled, but with controlled stress – and this strengthens your brain and psyche and carries the idea of being able to deal in a competent way with life and its difficulties.

How to Find this Safe Place

Human beings who have suffered from traumatic situations in most cases can tell you where they found a safe place in their psyche to survive the trauma. This safe place in the fantasy, the inner safe place, is different, according to each personality. Nevertheless, there is a kind of similarity: it is very often a concrete place in nature unknown to others, experienced vividly in fantasy, or even a place in the sky. Sometimes a helping figure is there: a protecting human being from the past, from dreams, from literature, from stories, or a helping animal. This safe place is a haven where traumatized people feel safe and contained. It offers a possibility for recovery. Sometimes this safe place appeared once in a dream and became adopted for fantasy-life. If it is possible to relate to this image in fantasy, it works as a kind of resource: people become quiet and are encouraged to face the difficulties in an new way. In Jungian psychoanalytic treatment of traumatized people, it is indispensable to create this haven of a safe place. If it is possible to create it in fantasy by means of imagination, the safe place can be found whenever it is needed. But it only works when the images are connected with emotions. If it is not possible to create the safe place in fantasy, it can be found in dreams and/or in a trusting relationship to an analyst. But also for those not in analysis, it is important to find a safe place. Where in the outer world do you feel really safe? Where in the inner world? You may also find a safe place in relationships to other people. Those plagued by anxiety are looking for other human beings for company and for mutual help. The need for attachment is constellated, the search for people you have confidence in begins. This is the possibility to together create a safe place in the outer world. This safe place does not mean that you split off the "dangerous" outer world, but that together you can better face the difficulties in the world: the steps which are necessary to change something. It means you become strong enough to deal with, and not to split off. To be attached means to enter into close committing emotional relationship in which you have to deal in a constructive way with conflicts.

To create a safe place and to attach to other people can occur together, for example, when talking about safe places, and the need to feel safe and secure.

During the Gulf War, many Swiss people felt very bad. The day after the war had begun, three different people in my analytic practice had been dreaming about bombs and cows. All three felt comfort in seeing the cows, in being in a cow barn: it was a protection against the bombs. What does that mean? These dreamers felt threatened by the bombs, and the dreams produced an image of safety, of calm. Cows represent the archetype of the nourishing quality of 'mother nature' and provided the dreamers with the emotion of retreat from the threatening world into a world of comfort and warmth. A fascinating experience began when one of the dreamers, a student, asked colleagues about dreams in connection with the Gulf War. He found several dreams with images of protection, images of safe places, such as going into the heart of Switzerland, into the mountains, for protection. These images can be seen as images of regression; however, they provided comfort. Sharing these dream images led to increased discussion with other people about what felt threatening, and they connected better than usual, so the panic lessened and they knew better what to do, became more creative, more resolved to keep control over their lives – at least in their own world. That meant to be capable of dealing with the danger.

There are terrorists in the world. Whatever is in the world is also a part of our psyche. It would be wise to get in touch with the terrorist side in ourselves. In killing the terrorists, it is likely that you become a terrorist yourself. If you create an aggressor, and you see all the destructive energies in this aggressor, you are a victim – and full of anxiety. You might feel strong and be willing to attack the aggressor, in order to create a safe place one day. But instead, you will create a spiral of violence. And you need the safe place now. It would be far better to get in contact with the aggressor and to engage in dialogue.

Some Problems Behind Destructivity

Let me explain this on an individual level. If you are angry because you feel that you have been treated in an unjust way, that you are not respected, and you know that no one will give you justice, you become destructive. The anger is telling you that something among the borders between people must be rearranged, that someone is inhibited in their survival instinct – and that means also psychological survival – or in the will to create something, is becoming dysfunctional. You want to destroy instead of changing something in the relationship. For to have a good argument, both of the opponents must have the same rights, there must be an indestructible intersubjectivity[6]. Both must be able to argue as long as it is clear what problem it is that is requiring a responsible response from both sides, and this until one is winning and the other is losing. This only creates new problems. What works on the level of the personality could also be a model for conflicts in the world. In other words: countries should be strong enough to enter a dialogue with each other. The prerequisite would be mutual respect and respect for the differences.

Propensity to violence is increasing. There are different reasons for this. One could be that human beings admire secret terrorist acts. The terrifying is close to the exalted.

[6] Habermas, Jürgen, *Vergangenheit als Zukunft*, Pendo-Profile, Zurich, 1990

There is nothing to be admired about violent acts: we should better admire what is good for life, not for death. Perhaps there is a reason beyond the political difficulties, beyond the problem of the world with religion (East) against the world without religion (West), beyond the injustice in our world and the increasing propensity to violence: death is repressed, and this seems to be a problem everywhere. Perhaps this problem is comparable to the situation at the time of Freud, when sexuality was suppressed; today it is death and dying, and old age that are suppressed. Instead of living in the face of death, people identify with death as the "not destroyable destroyer."[7] Instead of becoming more creative, cultivating love for life and facing death and dying, we admire destruction. We not only admire it, but even see it as necessary for protecting ourselves. Of course, if our borders are violated, we must clearly do everything to ensure that this does not occur again. But: the best prevention is determined dialogue – not war.

Fighting and winning belong to the field of the archetype of the hero. I propose a movement back to the field of the Mother archetype in its function of providing a safe place and connection, enabling an unconscious basis for a dialoguing brother- and sisterhood in the world: the sibling archetype.

Verena Kast is a professor at the University of Zurich, a training analyst at the Jung Institute, Zurich, and a past president of the IAAP. Some of her many book titles include: *Joy, Inspiration and Hope*; *A Time to Mourn* and *Sisyphus*.

[7] Williams, Mary, 1958, "The Fear of Death", Journal of Analytical Psychology, Vol. 3, pp. 157-165

From Wahhabism to Talibanism

Hechmi Dhaoui

I consider this text as a cry of pain expressing the suffering of the Arab-Moslem world to which I belong. This Moslem world has been "a chronic patient" since the 10th century. In order to analyze the regressive behavior of the Arab Moslem world, it will be necessary to review its social, political, and cultural evolution (or stagnation) over ten centuries. I will also examine the emergence of Arab nationalism and, finally, try to understand the origins of Islamism as a reaction to the failure of Arabism. The events of September 11th forced me to recognize that instead of love, the practice of contemporary Islam expresses primarily hatred.[1] I will analyze how hatred has come to *overshadow* the original Islam according to the holy texts (the *Koran*, the statements and the practices of the prophet).

The tragedy of September 11th has made only one positive contribution: the elimination of the indifference which wrapped the Moslem world. I will, therefore, try to speak about the causes of regression, hatred, and indifference in

[1] While writing this paper I have been in the midst of organizing an international symposium on the theme of love (scheduled for May 4, 2002). This paper and the symposium reflect my disappointment in Arab-Moslem culture after publishing *L'Amour en Islam* in June 2001. See Dhaoui Hechmi, *L'Amour en Islam*, l'Harmattan, Paris, 2001.

order to suggest an adequate solution. My arguments may appear a little too critical, especially as I will barely mention the involvement of the West. I consider that Arab Moslem intellectuals should first clean up their own backyards and efficiently analyze the behavior of their fellow citizens and governors in the context of a constructive self-criticism.

As for the Western world, I believe that they possess a sufficient number of intellectuals who can play the role of self-critic. See, for instance, the article of Noam Chomsky[2] in which he addressed a severe criticism to the foreign policy of the United States of America (although he had forgotten that the date of September 11th coincided with the twenty-eighth anniversary of the execution of Salvador Allende in Chile).

I will try in this study to demonstrate that the so-called "shock of civilizations" is misleading. Though the Arab Moslem world has its unique problems, we all share in the same human culture. When one culture, like an internal organ of the body, is sick, the whole *cultural* immune system reacts to cure the problem. I consider the actual experience of the Arab Moslem world to be pathological, and while I think that our pathology is our responsibility, I also think that the whole of humanity is called upon to find a therapy to treat the curse of terrorism. Terrorism is a psychosocial disease characterized by the bad management of internal emotions in the Arab Moslem world and by a loss of communication with the outside world; however, terrorism is not exclusive to the Arab Moslem world.

The relationships between Moslems themselves and between Moslems and foreigners are badly managed. We would certainly benefit from internalized ethics as described by Freud; ethics represent at least one antidote to human aggression (MC, 1978). Otherwise, the necessary therapy,

[2] Chomsky, Noam, "Le Nouveau Visage du Monde," in *Le Monde Diploma-tique*, 2001, n° 573

according to C.G. Jung, would "encourage regression, and this until it reaches the prenatal stage," where we would have to confront and analyze the imago of the mother.[3] There is a direct relationship between the reactive aggression of the Arab Moslem world and its relation to the archetype of the mother.

Our regressive attitude, thus far, has frozen the Arab Moslem world in a continual search for the Oumma (community of believers). "Oumma" carries the same etymological root as the "Omm" (mother), and would represent the Golden Age of Islam which all Moslems long for. The strength of this longing serves as a compensation for an inferiority complex. It would be far healthier for us to sacrifice our nostalgia.

In the last section of this paper, I will ask the Western world, in general, and the United States in particular, to understand and help the Arab Moslem world in its effort to abandon this regressive attitude and to re-emerge in history. It is necessary that the United States assume their responsibility since they are politically and financially the ally of Saudi Arabia which is the source of Islamism. Although the United Kingdom is politically and culturally the ally of the United States, it is also the protector of the Moslem fundamentalists who have found refuge in London. I find this a curious conjunction of opposites: the United States of America, whose political system is dominated by the Constitution, has very close relationships with two countries that do not have a constitution – certainly for different reasons but these two countries are, nonetheless, at the origin of the disaster of September 11th 2001.

Sandor Ferenczi[4] already mentioned in 1913 the possible application of the psychoanalytic model to social problems.

---

[3] Jung, C. Gustav, *Métamorphoses de l'âme et ses symbols*, George Editeur Genève, 1989, pp. 487, 546, 548 et 689

[4] Ferenczi, Sandor, "Importance de la psychanalyse dans la justice et dans la Société", in *Psychanalyse II*, Payot, Paris, 1970

Since social adaptation is a psychological process, Ferenczi considered that the sociology governing the individual's life in society and the laws to which the individual must adjust deserve a psychoanalytic analysis. The problem of the Arab Moslem world consists in a difficulty of adaptation to modernity (which means that it is a problem of sociology and law). There exists a confusion between the "temporal" and "spiritual," between the state and religion, and therefore, between human rights and divine right.

The Arab Moslem world lacks an ethical code that would naturally manage its instinctive aggressiveness. Only sublimation can help the Arab Moslem citizen to channel ("canalize" was Jung's original word) primitive instincts into activities that have a social value and away from religious zeal. A channel for sublimation is the only way to recover from longstanding regression. Hopefully, Arab Moslems will creatively adjust to our current epoch and abandon self-destructive nostalgia for an idealized past. A deep psychoanalysis of the Arab Moslem collective unconscious would be a great help, especially if accompanied by a "collective psychotherapy."

The "Shock of Civilizations"

Since the unfathomable terrorist aggression committed in New York and Washington on September 11th, only one reflection has disturbed me in all the debates that I either read or saw televised: it is the idea of the "shock of civilizations." The distinction between a dreamy, mystical, archaic, intuitive, irrational, and spiritual East with its Islam, and a pragmatic, materialistic, realistic, and emancipated West, may be clear and legitimate but by emphasizing these differences and underestimating our similarities, the distinction hurts chances for mutual understanding and dialogue. I remain persuaded that we are in both cases dealing with the same civilization: the Mediterranean civilization that started in the Fertile Crescent.

The Mediterranean is an "Interior Sea" that dug itself in the middle of the Old World, like a uterus that develops during the puberty of a girl. Before being culturally impregnated, this sea was virgin. Indeed, like the Virgin Mary, the Mediterranean Sea was immaculate until the appearance of human civilization in the so-called Fertile Crescent[5]. This Fertile Crescent is the region that spreads from Mesopotamia to the south of present-day Turkey.

We know neither how the first Mesopotamian cities were founded nor when and how cuneiform writing developed and spread in the form of bilingual Acadian tablets. Therefore, the process of fertilization of Mediterranean cultures that resulted from these factors has remained unknown. It is only at the end of the 2nd millennium B.C. that the linear alphabet, called "Phoenician," was invented in this fluvial island between the Tiger and the Euphrates. The Middle East has a key geographical position, since it is located at the crossroads of Europe, Asia, and Africa. This privileged position is certainly not due to luck, since it is in this region that metalwork techniques, the first writing, and the three monotheistic religions appeared. A similar phenomenon started almost simultaneously in Southeast Asia (China, India, and Indonesia) – a historical fact that currently finds its explanation in morphogenetics.

This civilization developed on the Mediterranean shores at the time of the Judaization of the region with a culture that remained dominant until 800 B.C. Jewish culture reached its peak under the reign of David and then of Solomon. The

---

[5] Braudel, Fernand, *Les mémoires de la Méditerranée*, Editions de Fallois, Paris, 1998

Jewish religion, set up by Moses the Egyptian who identified himself with his persecutor (the Pharaohs certainly knew a great civilization that remained local) and who was isolationist as was the Pharaoh's religion which did not accept other religions. In fact, "the Jewish Laws find their origins in Moses' Egyptian roots."[6] Later, those who were not Jewish were compelled to join monotheism through Christianity and Islam. In Judaism, the filiation or line of descent occurs through the mother, and a conversion is not recognized if the mother is not Jewish. We can surmise, therefore, that the archetype of the great mother influences both the Jewish and Arabic family and tradition.

Then came the neo-Assyrian time that lasted until 610 B.C. to be followed by the neo-Babylonian empire that lasted until 539 B.C. This latter civilization was completely swallowed by the Persian Empire until Alexander's accession to the throne of Macedonia in 332 B.C. The Greek warrior split apart the Persian Empire making the region into an Hellenic East until the individualization of the Parthian Empire in 60 B.C.

During the same period, the Phoenicians founded a coastal empire on the periphery of the Mediterranean. Later, the Greeks and the peoples of the Aegean Sea, and after them, the Roman Empire established the setting in which Christianity would spread. Finally, the advent of Islam – the second irrational reading of the Judaic religion – replaced the Christian religion on the southern coast of the Interior Sea and reached Andalusia.

In the beginning, the Arab preachers of Islam found no problems in spreading their religion as long as they headed westward. However, the situation was totally different when they tried to move eastward. Arab culture has left almost no traces in Asia or in Europe except Islam. In fact, the Arab's decadence started when they left Spain eastward to spread

---

[6] Malet, Maya, "Monothéisme et psychanalyse," *PUF*, 2001, p. 67

their religion in Europe. They experienced the same failure as all those who attacked the East (Alexander the Great, Napoleon, Hitler); those, on the other hand, who turned toward the West succeeded.

This was exactly what happened in 1492 when the Christians expelled the Moslems and the Jews from the Iberian Peninsula. If we consider that the strait of Djebal Tarak (Gibraltar) was the collar of the uterus (the Interior Sea), closed from both sides by the Islamic presence, it was re-opened and allowed the 3,000 years of Mediterranean civilization to deliver the New world, since it was at that time, in 1492, that the Western world discovered America.

What I have just tried to emphasize by searching for the origins of civilization is, in fact, the destiny of the Mediterranean Sea where we have, on the one hand, a rational reading of the monotheistic religion in the North and, in the South, an irrational reading and the same relationship with the Unique God which has created a tautological society with a fatalistic tendency.

In fact, these 3,000 years of Mediterranean civilization could have constituted the center of Freud's or Jung's interest; their original desire was to deal with archeology and to conduct research into a universal history. But because of a lack of means, and as a form of sublimation, they switched to research in the field of the individual's history, in other words, psychoanalysis. Even psychotherapeutic methods evolved differently around the Mediterranean with its cultural, racial, linguistic, religious, and climatic differences, having in common only what we can call "the natural aspect" or "Mediterranean spontaneity."

This setting allows me to develop a relatively optimistic approach, knowing that the expansion of Moslem Civilization to the South led this area to undergo a real regression. I am going to deal with these two ideas, hoping to reach the concept of the integration of knowledge and technology, which will be possible thanks to the concept of globalization, if, that is, globalization respects unique cultural differences. To accomplish this, I will deal with the scientific domain with which I am familiar and the therapeutic domain, and will, thus, avoid speaking about the astronomical, arithmetic, architectural, and other scientific contributions of the Moslem civilization.

Indeed, I will consider that the present therapeutic heritage has been the result of an accumulation of knowledge during the evolution of human civilization from the Mesopotamians until the Europeans, passing by the Phoenicians, the Greeks and Romans, and the exchanges with Far Eastern civilizations. All therapeutic achievement is the result of fertility as well as a mutual cultural enrichment.

We can consider that today's medical science, in general, and psychotherapeutics in particular, have progressed dramatically in the West; nevertheless, this progress is to a great extent the result of Europe's medieval heritage of Arab medicine that developed and transferred the medical knowledge of the ancient East: India, Persia, and China.[7] This sinusoidal movement that characterizes the history of medicine around the Mediterranean reminds us of Jung's cyclic time. The history of medicine is, in fact, a perfect example of the common destiny of the peoples surrounding the Interior Sea in a single civilization that goes beyond the diversity of beliefs and ways of expression of all Mediterranean cultures.

The Golden Age of Arab Moslem medicine is situated between the 8th and the 13th centuries with two important periods: from the 8th to the 11th century in the East and from the 10th to the 13th century in the Maghreb and in Andalusia. The organization of medical studies and of the practice of medicine were legislated in Baghdad at the beginning of the

[7] Rochdi, Rached, *L'histoire des sciences arabes*, Seuil, Paris, 1997.

10th century. Medicine remained very closely related to philosophy – hence, the title of "Hakim," assigned to the physician as well as to the wise man. This organization of the therapeutic art was adopted in the Western world following the model of the Moslem East and was accompanied by the multiplication of the places for the treatment of the soul called "Morestanes" (707 in Damascus and 765 in Baghdad and then everywhere in the Maghreb).

Therefore, from De Razès (Razi 850-923) to Avicenne (Ibnou Sina 980-1037), the list is too long to be able to mention all those who contributed significantly to the development of medical knowledge. For more details see *Pour une psychanalyse maghrébine*[8]. Let's switch to the period of Averroes (Ibn Rochd 1126-1198) and of Maimonide (1135-1204) who witnessed the end of the Golden Age of Arab Moslem medicine. They did their utmost to resist the decadence of their contemporaries. Indeed, Averroès was known for his universalism, his freedom of mind, and his combativeness in the defense of the ideas that made him renowned. He was so critical of his contemporaries that even his own people rejected him. Nowadays, he is recognized as the intermediary to the Western world who fostered the institution of the critical and rational mind preceding modernity.

In fact, it was starting from the 14th century that divisions and dissensions hurried the scientific, cultural, and especially medical decadence in the Arab Moslem world. This was especially the case of medicine, which regressed and sank in empiricism, charlatanism, chiromancy, and even the magic and the conjuration of the evil eye. It is with disdain that Khaldoun lbn (1332-1406), one of fathers of modern sociology, spoke about this medicine. The Prophet himself turned to these practices, whereas he considered medicine as a funda-

---

[8] Dhaoui, Hechmi, *Pour une psychanalyse maghrébine*, l'Harmattan, Paris, 2000

mental science exactly like theology. Ibn Khaldoun justified the Prophet by saying: "The prophet had a mission to teach us Divine Law, not medicine." He joins Rhazès who revolted against this behavior, rejecting spiritualistic prophetic medicine in order to protect and to give the pre-eminence to objective experimentation. This rational objectivity found the cultural setting where it could develop and express itself fully: the northern shore the Mediterranean.

It seems that Christian monotheistic culture is favorable to rationality and logos, a fact which can be explained by the absence of Jesus' father. This absence created in Christians a sense of something missing, and to fill this lack, they had recourse to logos which has generated a way of thinking and a Western way of life based on rationality, individualism, materialism, and the privileged left brain.

The kind of monotheism installed on the southern shore of the Interior Sea has been brought, on the other hand, by a prophet who did not know his mother. This led to a research of Eros and a mode of functioning based on the irrational right brain which is more spiritual, intuitive, collectivist, and communal, predisposed to obscurantism and expressing itself by means of maraboutism which is, even today, the most privileged place for psychotherapists. This maraboutism is actually a cult of the ancestors, a realization of a pagan pre-Islamic ritual.

This scientific regression continued into the Middle Ages when the Moslem world was shared by the colonial powers. The decadence reached its peak with the fall of the Ottoman Empire which was caused by two movements that replaced conscious habits of reflection: first, a return to obscurantist Islam, and secondly, a nationalism that spread from Turkey to all of the Arab Moslem world by Mustapha Kamel Ataturk. This nationalism was worsened by the installation of the state of Israel. I believe that the regression is curable, and I will try to develop this idea in the last section of this paper. I think that if Moslems let go of their nostalgia, they will be able to aspire to more rational thinking. This has already been taking place since the Arab Moslem Renaissance Movement (*Ennahdha*) of the end of the 19th century and the beginning of the 20th century[9]with reformers like Rifaa Tahtaoui, then Kacem Amine in Egypt, and Khéreddine, Abdelaziz Thâalbi, Tahar Haddad, and Bourguiba in Tunisia. On the other hand, thanks to the speed of communication, a possibility is offered to the Arab Moslem world to start making up for accumulated impediments and to integrate the leading scientific movements without fearing any Western hegemony.

Berlusconi did not understand that we share the same civilization; his Mussolinian heritage made him forget that the Greek and the Moslem knowledge reached Europe mainly through Salerne and Naples thanks to Constantine the Carthaginian. However, at the regional level, and according to the proper history of each region, this civilization has at times undergone internal evolutions which were appreciably very different to the point that one can meet today very modern minds in the East and very traditional ones in West. Therefore, I prefer to oppose Berlusconi to his compatriot Umberto Eco, who knows the history of civilization better than him.

To recapitulate, we have seen how the different exchanges and cultural interpenetrations around the Mediterranean have caused the birth of the New World after 3,000 years of civilization. Indeed, according to my metaphor, this Interior Sea constituted a uterus that has been impregnated by the Fertile Crescent in the Neolithic Era. This uterus gave birth in 1492 to the present America. As a consequence of the opening of its collar, the Moslems withdrew to the southern shore of the Mediterranean. This culture child took revenge, the first

---

[9] Charfi, Mohamed, "Islam et liberté," *Le malentendu historique*, Albin Michel, 1998

time, on the mother culture in 1991 when Iraq aggressively, incestuously attacked Kuwait as the culture girl.

To end this metaphor, I consider that what is happening today in Palestine is the visible aspect of deliverance by this effusion of blood between the Jewish and Arab brother-enemies that will end up in peace regardless of whatever sacrifices are required.

The "shock of civilizations" in the book of Samuel P. Huntington[10] did not take account of the anthropological reading of civilization. Huntington speaks about a lower-level culture, basing his analysis on secularism, democracy, and the Roman Right. I was shocked when I read his excellent theory on democracy.

First, he tried to show that the superiority of western civilization is obvious, which no one can doubt, and to describe the superficiality of its practice in the non-Western world. The West's most important asset is the great efficiency of its means of communication. Although Western communications technology encounters a strong resistance from non-Western dictatorial regimes, the oppressed peoples benefit from it, a fact that obviously frightens their regimes.

On the other hand, Huntington tried to minimize the contribution of the civilizations that preceded Islam, Islam being the translator of all the past knowledge that was later transmitted to the West. I would remind Huntington of a simple historic anecdote about the origin of the creation of Beit El Hikma (House of Wisdom) in Baghdad that was destroyed by the American bombardment of December 1998. It was the Caliph Al-Maamun (786-833), at the apogee of Abassite Islam, who ordered its construction so that researchers could translate all of Greek culture.

---

[10] Huntington, Samuel, *Le choc des civilisations*, Odile Jacob, 1997

The anecdote is that the decision was made following a dream of the Caliph in which he had the following discussion with Aristotle:

Caliph: Who are you?
Aristotle: I am Aristotle ...
Caliph: O wise man! Can I ask you some questions?
Aristotle: You can ...
Caliph: What is beauty?
Aristotle: What is beautiful in the intellect!
Caliph: What else?
Aristotle: What is beautiful for the law!
Caliph: What else?
Aristotle: What is beautiful around people!
Caliph: What else?
Aristotle: That's all!

Indeed, it was that dream that incited the regent to build that palace of knowledge where researchers worked under the direction of Hussein lbn-Ishâq (808-873) to translate all Greek books brought back to that place which was at the origin of the passage of ancient knowledge to the Western world.

I agree with Huntington when he says that it is individualism that characterizes the process of modernization in the Western world. In contrast, the Arab Moslem world has experienced a pathological mourning since the loss of Andalusia.

When he starts describing the communal conflicts in his chapter *"The Dynamics of the Wars of Civilizations"* and applies the phrase, "Wars of Identity," to ex-Yugoslavia, he only contradicts himself. Indeed, the Bosnian Moslems, who were not mosque-goers and did not mind wedding their daughters to the Orthodox Serbians or the Christian Croatians, became aware of their Moslem identity as a form of vital defensive regression, especially in reaction to the extremist Serbian and Croatian nationalists when they threatened them and committed genocide. I cite: "The Moslems of Bosnia had a very secular behavior." Was it possible for them to react otherwise in the face of Western aggression in which even UN soldiers participated? We cannot forget the massacres of Srebrenica's Moslems in the presence of French UN soldiers; this horror hauntingly reminds us of the massacre of the Palestinians in Sabra and Chatila in 1982 in Beirut by the Christian Militia that was under the protection of Sharon's army.

With the above in mind, I prefer to conclude this chapter with the quote from Morin Edgar: "The problems of domination, of opposition, of human barbarism...? Only reliance, real humanism, the conscience of earth-homeland would reduce ignominy in the world."[11]

The Consequences of De-colonization and the Cold War.

Actually, from the 14th century, the Arab Moslem world has experienced a progressive decline that resulted from the disorganization and the division of the Islamic Empire, a decline leading to its almost generalized colonization in the 19th century. It was in 1916 that the birth of the Arab Nationalism occurred when the English agents living in Saudi Arabia proposed to Cherif Houssein the creation of an Arabian empire stretching from the Gulf to the Ocean in return for their help to sweep the Ottoman Empire. This Arabism has, thereafter, evolved with the birth of the Arab League in 1945 and later with movements focused on political independence. This nationalism has been intensified by the Israeli-Arab conflict dating from 1948 and has been sustained by the Cold

[11] Morin, Edgar et Nair, Sami, *Une politique de civilisation*, Arlea, 1977, p. 245

War when the USSR tried to channel Arab Nationalism against the Free World's interests. Therefore, Arab Nationalism, which relies on Islam as a common value and denominator to all of the culturally different peoples, has survived because it has played a dynamic role in the struggle against invaders.

Certainly, the Arab Moslem countries have remained premodern, contrary to other countries that have found a balance between their local culture and the global culture. Arab States have remained attached to their cultural specificities and dependent on their previous status as colonized countries. They have adopted a defensive attitude toward the West which is nothing more than an inferiority complex. This is why Arab states keep turning their backs on any cultural communication; an opening would make them susceptible to new ideas about their rights as men and women and could lead to a democratic environment in their countries.

It is, indeed, necessary to stress the fact that during the post-colonial period most of the Arab Moslem countries were under the ascendancy of leaders who had been the heroes in their struggles for independence. These leaders could not resist their despotic evolution, as it was said by Jean Lambert[12]: "The tenacious cliché of the 18th century about the oriental despot and the coming centuries of confusion between the spiritual and the temporal, underestimates the nature of power and the succession of the Prophet." (*The Distributed God*).

These countries were in most cases under the aegis of a unique, authoritarian individual who presented himself as the new prophet and the leader of the Jihad against poverty and underdevelopment. Such leaders became demagogues (*Zaïm*) to the extent that, during the Cold War, they started rejecting

---

[12] Lambert, Jean, *Le Dieu distribué, une anthropologie comparée des monothéismes*, Certf, 1995, p. 254

the principles of human rights promoted by the Free World along with the excessive socialization preached by the Soviet Bloc.

The Arab leaders benefitted from the indifference of the two superpowers and used the opportunity to emphasize their cultural uniqueness in an Arab Nationalism that put the interests of the group and the community above those of the individual.

The most resourceful despot was Mustafa Kamal Ataturk, known as the "Secular Dictator" or the "Anti-Allah." His merit was to consider that "the politician who needs the help of religion to govern is a coward." This is the case of Saddam Hussein who has excelled in the field of cowardice by continuing to impose himself on his people and to lead his country to ruin. In fact, after having invaded Kuwait on a personal dictatorial initiative, he made his people pay for the damage he had caused while he led a regent's life. He has even outperformed bin Laden in cowardice, since he pretended to be a secular leader before turning into a fierce Moslem by adding the expression "Allah Akbar" ("God the Almighty") on his country's flag in the search for a Moslem coalition during the Gulf War. As for bin Laden, when he realized that most of the Moslem States refused to follow him, he tried to present himself as the defender of the Palestinian cause. Saddam, who continues to lead a campaign of religious awareness and piety, provoked a metamorphosis in his people's way of dressing: he has required his country's political leaders and officials to attend religious seminars, he has increased the number of religion-based newspapers, and he encourages research in Koranic sciences and Islamic jurisprudence. He has also invested in the campaign to encourage more and more women to wear the *hijab* (veil) and men to wear the *dajdajases* (long clothes).

Iran is another example of a country that has preached a certain modernism in a climate of repression. The Shah relied on his army to lead his country toward Western reforms. He believed that he was working for the benefit of his people by choosing a brutal and excessive Westernization. In fact, he provoked a defensive regression even among officers and soldiers, in addition to the people's resistance. They all united against him under the slogan "Allah'o Akbar" (God the Almighty). The Shah's oppression gave strength to Khoumeini's Islamic Revolution that rejected everything associated with the Western world.

Khoumeni proclaimed himself the Revolution's Prophet. This is how he set up the first Islamic Republic where, according to him, "faith is more precious that weapons." The Fundamentalist Iranian Revolution had just established itself when Iraq declared war on Iran on September 22nd, 1980, and thereby confirmed Khoumeini in his anti-American and anti-Western propaganda. Then, his regime knew a period of terror that had never been seen before, with real persecution of men and women when the fundamentalist revolution replaced the "Savak" by the "Savana," a politico-religious police which was far more subjective than the Shah's.

In the same region, there is another dictator who rules in the name of Islam, encouraged by the Free World as a participant in the Green Strip that resists the Soviet Union's invasion: it is "General-priest" Zia Ul-Haq who rules over Pakistan as an absolute dictator helped by an uncompromising martial law.

Most Moslem countries are ruled by different sorts of dictators like the President-Colonel Ali Abdullah Salah of North Yemen who took over in 1978 after eight years of civil war. Libya's Muammar Al-Khadhafi is a minor dictator who is indefinable. As for Boumediene in Algeria, he had exhausted his country's wealth as a result of a socialist bureaucratic policy. We cannot forget to mention Abdelaziz Ibn Saoud, King of Saudi Arabia, as a major Arab dictator, who can be referred to as "the Majestic Dictator." He rules over his country spiritually as well as temporally in a ruthless way. In Syria, General Hafedh Al-Assad has established a violent dictatorship under cover of an Arab Progressive Ideology (*The Bâath*) that he shared with Iraq, his brother-enemy.

It is impossible to list all of the Arab dictators because they are too numerous but I cannot omit to mention the father of pan-Arabism, Jamal Abdennaceur, who was known as the "Crusade Dictator" because of his fascination with the "Great Arabia." He was trained in a tough military school and did not try to conceal the fact that he considered Hitler as his model. He inevitably became the focus of Zionist anti-Arab propaganda since he wanted to throw the Jews into the sea. This arrogance led him to the loss of the first war against Israel in 1967. One positive result of his policy, however, was the dissolution of the Moslem Brothers' fanatic movement, although he did not do it for the sake of modernization but for a hegemonic purpose. He had the conviction that he embodied the future United Arabic world, exactly like Hitler when he said: "I am Germany." He "never managed to have a sane relationship with that feminine person that I call anima" said Jung[13]. I will develop this idea, which is also true for Islamists, in another chapter.

Nasser's ideology was, in fact, a Secular Arab Nationalism, inherited from the German Socialist Nationalism, which reigned over the whole Arab world with a few exceptions like Morocco of Hassan II and Mohamed V, Tunisia of Bourguiba, Jordan and Lebanon. Lebanon, meanwhile, has had to face the threatening invasion of the Syrian army.

It is the same Arab Nationalism that has created the fear of the Saudi regime for its own existence in an Arab hegemony

[13] Jung, C. Gustav, *Jung parle, rencontres et interviews*, Buchet / Chastel, 1995

although it is based on a legalistic Sunnite Wahhabite Islam-ism. To further its ambitions, the Saudi regime has been financing International Islamism. It has even established an implicit alliance with Zionism directly or indirectly through the United States against the common enemy of this creeping Nasserism and against its successors Khadafi, El-Assad, and Saddam Hussein.

Up to now, there has been a tacit alliance between Israel and Saudi Arabia for their survival (well described by Alex-ander Adler in *International Mail*). Today, Saudi Arabia and Israel are working hand in hand to try to solve the Palestinian problem. What frightened the Saudis was Nasser's statement: "In order to achieve Arab unity and socialism, first, we have to fight the Arab reactionaries, then get rid of the imperialist bases in the Middle East, after that get rid of the economic influence of the Western world and put an end to the imperi-alist hand-stake on the Arab oil reserves."[14] This was a speech that awakened the suspicion of the United States and was at the origin of their alliance with the Islamists.

The Islamists have held the secular Arab regimes responsi-ble as the cause of the spectacular defeat of the Six-Day War. In fact, it was a defeat that could only remind the Arab conscience of the loss of Andalusia in 1492. Psychologically speaking, the suffering would be unbearable if the Arabs came to lose Palestine and Jerusalem, exactly as it was when they lost Grenade and Seville, which was an awful tragedy that triggered the regression of the Arab Moslem world. This loss of Andalusia urged the Arabs to exit history. Since then, they have been in search of the path that would bring them back to the possibility of playing a role in global human dynamics.

The Arabs have not managed to emerge from archaism to modernity because of the oppressive regimes that have pre-vented them from evolving toward democracy. We have actu-

---

[14] Rouleau, Eric, *Israël et les Arabes, le 3è combat*, Le Seuil, 1967

ally been the cause of our own misfortune since we have remained attached to a stereotype in which objectors and marginal people are considered as traitors, often abusively condemned. Bin Laden has certainly caused great harm to the West, but, on the other hand, his recent deed threatens to destabilize several Arab regimes by affecting tourism and foreign investments. Think only of Egypt which is facing serious economic problems due to the decline of its tourist industry and the fact that its population increases by one million every eight months.

Bin Laden could have emerged from any Arab country because he is the result of the generalized tyranny in this part of the world where there is no place for politics. It is in this part of the world that Socrates' statement more than 2,400 years ago finds its application: "There where there is tyranny there is no policy." I will add that tyranny gives birth to terrorism. Indeed, the Arab regimes, without exception and for a long time, have been (with the consent of the Western world) at the origin of new fanatic religious movements. These movements, which are opposed to the despotism of the Arab regimes, are struggling for their recognition. All the Arab regimes excel in finding ways to destroy enlightened forces by being against anything emanating from civil society, preventing all freedom of speech and considering the defenders of men's rights as enemies who must be eliminated. This is how these regimes have encouraged the fundamentalists, who are themselves against nationalism and democracy, to prosper.

Tunisia can be considered as the most westernized Arab country. Since 1859, Tunisia has had a Constitution which was revised in 1958, two years after its independence. This Constitution was supposed to adjust and to guarantee the political proceedings but it became an instrument of repression in the hands of the President of the republic. Bourguiba violated the Constitution a first time when he established himself as President for life. Today, the Constitution is being violated a second time by his successor who wants to extend his term of office and guarantee himself a total and eternal immunity. Actually, this example shows well that, in Arab countries, only the head of the state can enjoy freedom. All those who work in the "political field" are given legitimacy by him and no one else; this is also true for so-called "legal opposition parties."

If you consider all Arab regimes one by one since their independence, you will notice that they have been governed by leaders who refused to "leave the throne" before their physical deaths. As these regimes are backed up the West, and especially by the United States, the Arab people can only be angry at America that is at the same time the protector of the state of Israel. These two factors – the support of oppressive regimes and the protection of Israel – are, in fact, the origin of Arab peoples' demonization and hatred for the United States.

As all these regimes do not have any political ethics, they allow themselves to say things that are apparently acceptable and to pass laws which are often less acceptable. Such an absurd situation urges individuals or groups who want to play a political role to react but they are then ruthlessly repressed by the regime's security police. These oppressive regimes do not hesitate to resort to imprisonment, torture, and even murder, and the discontent of the people increases. Among the repressed, some manage to flee their countries and find refuge in the free world where they may organize themselves into terrorist groups whose aim is to take revenge on the United States.

I consider Arab Nationalism as the heir of Nazism and Turkish nationalism. It is in fact a nationalism that is in search of an Arab unity with a strong emphasis on the Arab community (*Oumma*) and with the Israeli-Arab conflict as a focal point for grievances.

Arab Nationalism is probably the reason why all the Arab leaders decided to support Saddam Hussein against the United States before the Arab League Summit of March 2002. In fact, the only thing Arab leaders share with Saddam Hussein is tyranny. They even agreed to betray the Palestinians by exchanging – by giving up – Arafat in favor of Saddam. They have even conspired with Sharon by putting Arafat and his people in his hands. The American attitude was characterized by a cynical neutrality.

Such policies will only lead to the reinforcement of the position of nationalist extremists and Islamists in the whole Arab world. Open-minded people and modernists will be the ones to pick up the pieces. On the Israeli side, this policy seems logical as they work only for their own interests. The United States does not appear to profit from the lessons of the past. Americans, therefore, will keep asking themselves the eternal question: "Why don't they like us?"

We Arabs are the real cause of our misfortunes because we still suffer from the psychological complex of a former colonized people which makes us face our problems with reactionary attitudes. This complex of inferiority is at the origin of our denial of "the other," our rejection of everything emanating from the Western world, and the confusion between modernity and everything contemporary. It is this very complex of inferiority that was at the origin of the regression that Algeria experienced after independence in a desperate hope to belong to the Arab community.

I have chosen to deal with Algeria because their example illustrates the Arab leader's state of mind. The Algerian relationship to the rest of the Maghreb is not due to hazard. After independence, Algeria opted for an excessive Arabization. But, unlike its two neighbors, Morocco, with the "Karaouïn" University and Tunisia with the Zitouna University, Algeria did not dispose of a sufficient number of teachers; consequently, in 1962, it turned to Egypt. At that time Jamal Abdennaceur was struggling against the fundamentalist Islamists. The situation in Algeria provided an opportunity for Jamal Abdennasser to get rid of the Islamists by sending 18,000 Arabic teachers there. It is, in fact, these Egyptian Islamist teachers who formed a whole generation of obscurantist fundamentalists in Algeria. Once again, the funds came from Saudi Arabia through the "IsIamiste internationale" whose rotating plate is in London, in the United Kingdom. Of course, the poor socialist management in Algeria made it possible for the corrupted army to take power.

It is once again the longing of the Algerians to join this hypothetical Arab Community (Oumma) that prepared their downfall toward a radical Islamism that is also in search of the Islamic Community (Oumma). This constitutes a double collective communal blemish, a regressive search for the mother. This continual search for the mother constitutes a collective defect, and the Arabs go beyond this defect by searching for a "great mother" (Oumma).

This is how we have been witnessing a progressive evolution of the Arab Moslem individual as a member of a community that is cloistered in traditional search of a heritage (*turath*) whose merits are painfully exaggerated. This is the typical context in which fundamentalist ideas flourish.

In the 60s and 70s, some mosque-goers imposed themselves as God's spokesmen even though in the Moslem religion there must be no mediator between the believer and his God. They progressively replaced the heroes of Arab Nationalism who were in a situation of economic, political, and cultural failure. The conflict has been heightened by the failure of Arab nationalists to find a solution to the Palestinian problem in spite of the promises that they kept repeating.

The breakdown of Arab nationalism's structure opened the way to the hegemony of Islamism, as second heritage of the

Arab Moslem culture. This culture has indeed brought a legislation (*Charia*) that can oppose itself to any form of secularism (although I think that secular law must respect religion since religion should concern only the individual in his relationship with his creator).

Islamism, the Offspring of Arabism

Today, Islam is imposing itself in Arab countries as a religion and as public legislation to the extent that the speeches preaching the Islamization of modernity have become frequent. This is how one can understand the Islamists' dual language: they have the talent for summoning up an imaginary opposition (characterized by a liking for conflicts, exclusion, and sectarianism) or an imaginary unity (characterized by a liking for analogy, communion, rallying, and integration). But never can the Islamists find themselves in an imaginary alliance (characterized by dialectics, communication, tolerance, and cohabitation).

This is the second strategic mistake made by the West (and the United States in particular) in assessing Islamization. The West thought they could stop the progress of the Red Communist wave with the help of the Green Strip that the Asian Moslem countries constituted. It was an apparently convincing project since its realization did not require any contribution from the American taxpayer. The necessary funds were supplied by Saudi Wahhabism, which is the principal ideologist of Islamism. This ideology is based on the theories of the thinkers (*Oulamas*) of El Azhar in Egypt who separate couples through religious legislation and who legitimize women's lower status in the Arab peninsula.

This Wahhabism, that started in the 18th century, turned into obscurantist ideology of Islam as a result of a complete misinterpretation of the founding texts: the *Koran* and the Prophet's statements. The Wahhabists have been the cause of many misinterpretations of the original religious texts because of their reactionary minds. It was, in fact, the encounter between Mohamed Ibn Abdel-Wahab and Mohamed Ibn Saoud in 1745 on the Prophet's arid land that gave birth to this Islamist drift caused by a rigid Islam that interprets the founding texts literally. This is how an ultra-legalist Sunnite Islam based on orthodox legislation was born.

This interpretation of the religious text which forbids music, poetry, and jewelry did not exist even in the days of the Prophet who used make-up (*khol*) and perfume. As for music, it is necessary to see what El Farabi (872-950) says about it. Al-Ghazali (1058-1111) who is the proof of Islam said "music imitates nature and the song of birds that belong to creation; forbidding it, is, therefore, against creation."[15]

Abdelwahab, the religious man, and Saoud, the warrior, made of this rigid Islam a new ideology. The former interpreted the Prophet's deeds in the way that suited Saoud who in return could retain enough power to protect his ally, Abdelwahab, the legal administrator. They even dared to destroy all the tombs including those of the Hachemites (the Prophet's tribe) who are the legitimate heirs of the Prophet and whose descendants govern Jordan. This was done in order to get rid of historically legitimate competition. For this, they did take into account the Prophet's Hadith that allows the visit of the dead after having forbidden it: "I had forbidden you the visit of tombs; now, visit them." (Moslem)

This is an example among so many others that show how, for ideological reasons, they dared divert the founding religious principles against clear Koranic verses, like the verse 21 of the sourate XXXIII of the Koran that says: "You have in

[15] Al Ghazali, Abu Hmed, "Reviviscence des sciences religieuses," *Maison du livre scientifique*, Beyrouth, 1992

Allah's prophet an admirable example," without taking account of the verse 115 of the sourate IV that says: "The Moslems who disobey the prophet and follow another path than that of believers shall be responsible for their acts and shall burn in the fire of Hell." Indeed, Saudi Arabia is the only country where the existence of cemeteries is prohibited, so visits to the dead are prohibited for purely political reasons.

These Salafi Islamists were very often against the Prophet's statements that encourage the renovation of Islamic practices according to time and space. The "Ijtihad" (interpretation) that should take into account time and space permits a certain suppleness in the interpretation of the holy texts. In this context, it says: "In every century, God will send to the Islamic community someone who will modernize the Moslem religion." This took place in the 19th century thanks to the cultural and social renewal started by Mohamed Abdou (1830-1897) and Jamel-Eddine al-Afghani (1849-1905) who wondered whether it was possible to pull the Moslem civilization out of its historic dead-end and to give it back the place it deserved. They hoped to rid Arab culture of its sense of failure and to transform the Age the Decadence and create in its place a certain contemporary consistency.

In its Salafism (nostalgic obscurantism) the Saudi Wahhabism considered this modernizing approach as an infidel's diabolic invention whose aim was to break the unity of the believers' community. Then the Saudis accused Arab Nationalism of being responsible for the unforgettable defeat of the Six-Day War. Finally, they empowered the Moslem Brothers' movement founded in March 1925, in Low Egypt, by two teachers: Hassan al-Banna (1906-1948) and Sayed Qotb (1906-1966). It is a movement that legitimates violence against any regimes judged impious. From the beginning, the Brothers' movement has benefitted from the political and financial support of King Faycal of Saudi Arabia, under the pressure of the Wahhabites. The Moslem Brothers' movement also received support from the American intelligence services that considered this war machine as a free opportunity to fight against the more and more pro-Soviet Arab Nationalism, especially since February 1958, the date of the creation of the United Arabian Republic with the union between Egypt and Syria.

It is this Moslem Brothers' movement that generated all the other groups in Moslem countries where they organized themselves according to the political specificities of their regions. This is how the movements of the "Islamic tendency" started in Tunisia and then evolved into a movement called "Ennahdha" whose charismatic chief, Rached El-Ghannouchi, can be considered as the prototype for the ideological metamorphosis of other group chiefs. In fact, he had first been a Nasserian Arab Nationalistic, then Baathist for 17 years before he adopted the Moslem Brothers' ideology that he tried to adapt to the Tunisian context. In Algeria, we find the FIS, Hisbou Allah (*Hezbollah*) in Lebanon, Hamas in Palestine, and the Jihad Islamism almost everywhere in the Moslem world. In Pakistan, we find the Islamic Jamaat which is a fundamentalist movement created by Maulana Maoudidi in 1941. Its ideology places the political and military movements as priorities to submit all the believers to the Islamic Law "Chariaa."

Maoudidi even considers that the Arab countries are corrupted. It is his movement that was at the origin of the Rushdi affair from the Koranic schools of Pakistan that attracted the attention of Khoumeini with the street demonstrations. It is one of the most virulent movements that views the jihad (seen as a real Holy War and not just as a spiritual effort) as essential to defend Islam.

All these fundamentalist Islamist movements, and others that share their objectives, are based on an ideological interpretation that distorts the meaning of the founding texts. This allows them to impose their own geopolitical vision and to wield an armed hand that they can use like a Damocles' sword against their ideological objectors.

This is how they dared denature the spirit of Islam by distorting some Sourates to allow themselves either to claim or to legitimize their jihad. Islam, however, considers that peace is the basis of communal life, whereas war is just an exceptional solution. The Koranic verses that carry this significance are numerous; here are some of them:

Verse 256 of the sourate II:
"Religious practices cannot be imposed; straightforwardness is henceforth very distinct from insanity."

Verse 40 of the sourate XII:
"Communication is your duty, judgment is ours."

Verse 125 of the sourate XVI:
"Preach the path of your Lord through wisdom."

Verse 29 of the sourate XVIII:
"Say: The truth emanated only from our Lord. Believe it or deny it."

Verses 21-22 of the sourate LXXXIII:
"Preach, for them, you are just the one who preaches, not the one who rules."

Verse 6 of the sourate CIX:
"You have your religion, I have mine."

In these Koranic examples, God addresses himself to the Prophet who applied them during his life to respect the monotheist religions. As for verse 60 of the sourate VIII that fundamentalists mention to give a purpose to the jihad, it says: "Prepare as many alert horses and weapons as you can to frighten God's enemy." This verse has no other objective than dissuasion and can by no means legitimize terrorism, especially since the following verse speaks about peace: "If they are for peace; be for it, without losing faith in God."

This is how the serious misinterpretations made by the Salafist Fundamentalists appear among the Islamists, changing a call for peace into an aggressive, terrorist ideology against Islam's precepts that clearly call for an exclusively defensive attitude.

All of these conceptual drifts and corruptions of the way of being a Moslem are the consequence of the Moslem Laws (*Fiqh*) made by men through history that have unfortunately become more important than the founding texts themselves. To my sense, it is at this level that we will find a solution by asking ourselves questions relative to what is licit and what is illicit with a view to the cult (*ibadats*) and to transactions (*mouamalats*).

We should take into account what is useful in our time without misinterpreting the *Koran* and the Prophet's authentic statements. At the same time we can apply the human scientific contributions like philosophy, sociology, anthropology, and psychology that will allow us to understand the symbolic content of the *Koran* which is full of parabolas of signs (verse: *aya*). This is what God calls for when he says in verse 24 of the sourate XIX: "Haven't you seen how God expresses (under the shape of a parabola) a beautiful word similar to a beautiful tree whose root is strong and the branch (point) skywards." Besides, I consider my claim to ideologists of Islam or even to those who consider themselves as the protectors of its practice, as being legitimate because it is based on the "Hadith," the Prophet's statements that have been reported by Boukhari as well as by Moslems according to whom "whoever makes use of 'Ijtihed' and finds a right solution will have two rewards; whoever makes use of 'Ijtihed' and finds a wrong solution will have only one reward."

Therefore, this "hadith" gives the legislator the right to error, which is more likely to happen when interpreters do not recognize the contributions of modern human sciences.

But we are confronted with a strong resistance and even a marginalization of all those who have tried to bring a new theological enlightenment. Even the rare innovators of the Arab Moslem revival of the 19th century, like Tahar Haddad, Ali Abderrazak, Taha Houssein, Mohamed Taha, Jamaleddine al-Afghani, and Mohamed Abdou, have remained very limited at the level of the impact of their ideology. Their ideas reached and convinced only a limited number of people. Some of them were even persecuted and harassed by the official religious structures of our dictatorial regimes.

I take the liberty to be critical vis-à-vis my Islamic culture and not Islam as a religion because I remain persuaded that it is the only means to be able to come out of our historic dead-end. In fact, I remain persuaded that the Moslem world is closed to any modern values and that it is unable to practice them entirely because of its intellectual weakness in an atmosphere of political authoritarianism inherited from German National Socialism through the Turkish Nationalism which constitutes the Axis with Hitler. Cultivating "Islam as religion" is, in my opinion, the only way for Islam to avoid being despised not only by the non-Moslems but also by its followers.

It is absolutely necessary to bring the Moslem elite to adopt a different position by considering that the Moslem community is experiencing a decline because the initial religious purity has been spoiled. The only way for Moslems to avoid incomprehension, condescension, and jingoism is by a critical position that will allow an open rational approach to technology and modern geopolitics that was once a source of pride during the Golden Age of Islam.

It is really time for us to pull ourselves together and for the Arab Moslem world to face its reality and to draw the most painful conclusions if necessary; only this cay can we aspire to a better future. We also need to face the reality that the average income per capita in the historic region of Islam does not exceed the world's average of 7,350 dollars, whereas it is 34,260 dollars in the United States, and 19,320 dollars in Israel. Nevertheless, the Moslems, or rather those who take the liberty to speak in the name of Islam, are capable of an immeasurable energetic effort when it comes to condemning, in the name of Islam, all those who dare disagree with them or suggest a new interpretation or understanding of their religious practice. This was also true for the Shiites when Khoumeini made Salman Rushdi's murder licit; and for the Sunnite when they legitimized the murder of the poet Fouda in Egypt. This has nothing to do with what has happened in the other monotheistic religions where books like Diderot's *Nun* or Spinoza's *Tractatus Theologico-Politicus* and Feuerbach's *The Essence of Christianity* have not been forbidden even though they developed a sharp criticism of their own religions.

Moslems become united when they are called to react against an individual whose speech is a little rational – as if there were only one theoretical Islam that represents the absolute truth. Islam has always been manifold. One finds a Sunnite Islam and a Shiite one cohabiting with an confraternal Islam and a mystic one, in parallel with a so-called political Islam, each with subgroups, each one with its specificities.

Even at the level of faith one finds the historic and primitive differentiation between a Motazalite Islam and an Achârite one, in addition to the four major tendencies inspired each from an Imam.

This obvious and reactionary Moslem solidarity draws its legitimacy from the "hadith" of the Prophet who says: "Help your brother whether persecuted or persecutor"; but they forget that when someone asked the Prophet how he could accept to help an oppressor, he answered: "It is up to you to prevent him from persevering."

It is this kind of regressive and reactionary behavior that has weakened and overcast the political, economic, and cultural image of Islam almost everywhere in the world. Besides, Islamism has tarnished the Mohammedan religion more and more. That is why I consider that, while denouncing their lies as well as their practices, I am not attacking Islam as a religion; on the contrary, I am trying to diagnose the fundamentalist evil in order to find an adequate treatment and eradicate it, hence to purify the body of Islam. When dealing with the Islamists, it is always good to use the necessary precision because they are particular and totalitarian people who believe in the principle that stipulates: "If you are not with me, you are against me." Their aim is to marginalize all Arab Moslem intellectuals who do not share their restrictive interpretations. And here I summon all intellectuals to remain heedful and to avoid falling into the trap of self-censure, the trap of avoiding topics held to be taboo – like everything related to religion. For this, it will be necessary to organize our struggle and to place it in the service of morality, ethics, and the common good.

Let's not forget one example: when Khoumeini made his "fatwa" (judgment) against Rushdi without having read his book, he tried to push the Moslem world in an ultimate process of denial of the West. Unfortunately, a large current of opinion in the Islamic world identified itself with the executioner rather than the victim. This fact caused a widespread condemnation of Iran and through it the entire Moslem world for their inquisitorial procedure of apostasy that prevented, in the name of community beliefs, the individual from existing outside the indivisible and sacred unity myth. According to this myth, the individual can exist only within a community of believers. The fanatic Islamists forget that by condemning an individual for his ideas, they reject the principle according to which a society is nothing if not a group of free individuals. On the other hand, they are capable of taking advantage of the principle of tolerance by asking for the respect of their resentment and their right to hate "the other" because their identity has been tarnished or injured. Bernard Lewis captured our predicament that began in the 19th century when he said[16]: "Finally the fundamentalists struggle against two enemies, secularism and modernity ... the struggle against modernity is neither conscious nor explicit and aims at all the process of change."

I have developed all of these contradictions between the founding texts and their ideological interpretation, on the one hand, and the fundamentalist movement's "doubletalk," on the other, and especially that of the Saudi Wahhabism that is trying to compel recognition in the Moslem world now that it feels menaced in its leadership by the Iranian Islamic Revolution.

The Soviet invasion of Afghanistan was a godsend for the Wahhabists, who did their utmost to help the Moujahidins free the Moslem Soil from the Soviets. The Wahhabists were represented there by Osama bin Laden, who was backed by the American Secret Service. They had the opportunity to spread their rigid and regressive view of an intolerant Islam that does not have anything to do with its origins. Tragically, the Americans only gave birth to the Talibans that I consider as cannon fodder, symbol of the Asian Islam inspired from the Saudi Wahhabism. Indeed, there is no objective difference between the practices of the Moujahidins of Commander

[16] Lewis, Bernard, *Le retour de l'Islam*, Gallimard, 1986

Messaoud and the Talibans of Moallah Omar. It is enough to see the woman walking in her "burqua," like a shadow, exactly like 50% of the population of Saudi Arabia where women have just acquired, under international pressure, the right to have an identity card. International opinion pointed out the Islamic practices of the country which is responsible for the existence of the Talibans whose government has been recognized only by Saudi Arabia, the United Arabian Emirates, and Pakistan where they had been trained with Saudi funds. This Wahhabite Islam stood out not only by a retrograde Islamization in Asia, but it also stood out by a very particular Moslem practice in Black Africa where the Wahhabism gave birth to what is called in the African continent the "Talibés." They are also students in the Koranic schools controlled by the Marabout that replaces the Moallah. The characteristic of the Wahhabite African Islam is that it has made the Talibés real slaves at the disposal of the Marabout who sell them to plantation owners. The Wahhabites are – and thanks to the money of the Saouds with whom they share the power – behind all terrorist actions that take place in the world and for whose actions Islam is held responsible. Among these actions, there is the tragedy of the World Trade Center in 1993, the massacre of 62 tourists in Luxor in 1997, the attempts of Nairobi and Dar Essalam in 1998, the American ship in 2000 in Yemen, September 11th in New York and Washington, without forgetting the 100,000 Algerians killed by the GIA, and the kamikaze attacks made by the Islamic Jihad and Hamas in Palestine that prevented President Yasser Arafat from carrying out the peace negotiations.

Suicide operations are completely forbidden in the Prophet's hadiths according to a clear interpretation of the founding text. Once again the Islamist and Wahhabist ideology has encouraged a practice which is completely forbidden by Islam. The prophet's hadith is very clear on this point: "The one who gives himself death with whatever means, shall be punished with the same means. How dare he eliminate something that does not belong to him?" This is a Moslem principle according to which the human body belongs to God who entrusts us with it; our role as human beings is to protect it and never harm it (Moslim). This is how Wahhabism, instead of respecting our bodily integrity according to Moslem spiritual norms, tries rather to prevent Moslems from caring for their bodies by obliging men to wear beards and women to wear burqas in order to remind them of their total subjugation.

This is what should be kept in mind about the role played by the Wahhabists in the International Islamism that attempts to indoctrinate Moslems: Islamism would persuade Moslems to put away individual claims and to integrate themselves into the community of believers according to an old model, nostalgically revitalized without being spiritually authentic. This is, in fact, a way of preventing the Moslem world from progressing.

Indeed, the Moslem Empire, that was founded on religious principles in the 7th century, can not possibly be revived on the same principles in the 21st century. Especially today, Islam is no longer a project of society but rather a claim for an identity that puts aside the spiritual ethics meant to raise the human being from his animal status. Since identity is a labile and changing experience according time and place, it is incapable of being the basis for the construction of a modern society with the institutions to sustain a modern state facing more and more complex challenges to people socially, culturally, and politically. Instead of this, the Wahhabists have created in central Asia a terrorist machine which is much more important than the Talibans; it is the Hisbou Attahrir el Islami (party of the Islamic Revolution) that currently rages in the Moslem Republics of the ex-Soviet Union in Central Asia.

The Psychological Profile of an Islamist Fundamentalism

All fundamentalists share the same ideas with bin Laden who represents the prototype of the Islamist. He could not have become a leader without the financial and political support of Saudi Arabia and the American intelligence services.

All the fundamentalists are incapable of replacing their self-centeredness with a constructive self-criticism. They remain in a state a self-satisfaction which is at the edge of psychosis. They keep considering themselves as eternal victims without wondering about the reality. They live in an imaginary world which is controlled by impulses toward pleasure and security. The Islamists consider that the killers they appoint are "heroes" and the kamikazes are "martyrs," and they do this without taking into account the foundations of Moslem religion.

Fundamentalism is nothing but a denial of reality. Even their "intellectual" elite read only their own literary productions which reflect a pathological narcissism accompanied by a total denial of the intellectual debates that have been going on for ten centuries. This confirms the idea that the Arab Moslem world is living on the margin of history. In fact, the Islamists refuse to attend to modernity by imposing fascism against democratization.

Fanatics can even be compared to drug addicts, or to addicts "hooked" on an ideology derived from Islam. This ideology constitutes a real drift in relation to the founding texts of Islam. Their speeches convey nothing but racial hatred towards "the other" and express contempt for minorities, women, and children; in addition, they marginalize all the speeches that are different from theirs.

It is true that our culture does not tolerate casting doubt over the established order, and therefore, marginalization is a recurrent problem. Consequently, Moslems never take into account the psychological development of their children; they just reproduce the same culture by transmitting to children the heritage of their ancestors in order to give them the possibility of a better integration in their society. This is a sociological model of education.

Thus, a person who reproduces the same culture will consider every new opinion as a transgression of the social and communal law.

Fanatics deny the hatred they bear towards individuals who want to free themselves from patriarchal influence and to become responsible and independent. These fanatics express only one need: the father-leader embodied by the imam is, for them, the only person capable of protecting them because they feel like children after their psychological regression.

However, when a religious man invests his entire libido in God, his ego is drained of its vital energy, which generates the educational requirements characterizing the anal stage of development. Especially in our culture, the anal-sadistic stage lasts longer than recommended in psychoanalytic, developmental literature. It seems that our culture has a large-scale potential to foster paranoid thinking. What a fate!

As we know, it is during the anal stage that the conflict between the individual and his environment reaches its climax. This conflict is characterized by the utmost sadistic and masochistic attitudes. And it is here that the interventionist and the rigid educational practices interfere to psychologically castrate the child, which causes irreversible damage to the child's personality. This is obviously the case of the interventions of the father and those of the educator, "Moaddeb," who, like the principal of a Taliban's Madrassa, represents, in fact, an educational reference. These Koranic school educators, called Moallahs in Afghanistan and Pakistan, are called Marabout in Africa where they produce Talibés who are sold as slaves on plantations. These Talibés suffer from a feeling of guilt when they do not obey the Marabout, who is feared because he is the symbol of the father's power. The education that I have characterized as interventionist and rigid has proved to be literal and legalistic especially when it comes to religious education. There is no room for any reflection or speculation about the significance (the *batin*) of the founding texts. This analysis leaves no doubt as to the capacity of Wahhabist Islamism to produce Talibans in Afghanistan as cannon fodder and Talibés in Africa as slaves. The "influence of the Wahhabist authority which is embodied by the soberness of its religious building" according to Roger of Pasquier[17], does not reflect the reality of Wahhabism. This Islamism that bears a total hatred toward democracy and toward those who call for negotiation and discussion in order to support the value of individual responsibility. Islamists prefer to produce reactionary ideas and to remain incapable of communicating. They avoid the act of thinking like the plague because debate could permit the pacific coexistence of opposite opinions which might show that they are wrong.

I think that it is the long passage of the ordinary Moslem through the anal-sadistic stage during his education that causes the appearance of a form of masochism symbolized by the religious person's self-denial through suicide (kamikaze, suicide bombing). This death allows him to continue his regression even beyond the anal stage to the intra-uterine life (fetal) that represents a promise of eternal beatitude.

In fact, it is according to Jung a regression that goes beyond the mother to reach the "Great Mother" who repre-sents this Oumma (mother) or community of believers who is in reality an archetypical mother who is still enduring the mourning of lost Andalusia. This situation has been revived

[17] de Pasquier, Roger, *L'islam entre tradition et révolution*, Edition Tougui, 1997

154

and stimulated at the level of the collective unconscious by the threat of losing Jerusalem in the Israeli-Palestinian conflict. It is probably this mourning that urges suicide bombers to search for this "maternal myth in which one changes and from which one can start again." (Elie G. Humbert[18])

History identifies a predecessor of bin Laden who belongs to the collective unconscious of the Moslem: Hassan Sabbah, who in 1065 withdrew to Halamut to transform his canyon-enclosed prairie into a terrestrial paradise for his (*Hachachin*), the kamikazes of that time, in search of eternal life under the effect of narcotics. These people attacked and killed for their chiefs without taking into account their victim's religion.

This is also the case of Osama bin Laden and of several other Moslem fundamentalists. Of course, he has some specific features arising from his personal unconscious. He was born in 1956 in Mecca, the holy place of Islam. His father belonged to a great Yemeni family from Hadramaout, a very ancient city. His Saudi mother was one of the 12 wives of his father. He is, therefore, the only son of a Saudi mother among 52 brothers and sisters. He pursued his engineering studies, and graduated in 1979 from the University of King Abdulaziz in Jeddah. His friends described him as a deeply religious person but "full of self-importance" which can be the appearance of his narcissism or megalomania.

Family business put him in contact with Turkish businessmen in Istanbul, which was on the route of the Arabs recruited to go to Afghanistan to fight the Soviets. This is where he was contacted by the CIA with which he established strong ties. He decided to join the Afghan resistance in the battlefields in 1980. He remained in Afghanistan until the departure of the Soviets in 1989.

---

[18] Humbert, Elie G., "Le prix du symbole," in *Cahiers de psychologie jungienne* n° 25, 1980, "Le sacrifice," pp. 31-45

In Afghanistan, he became friends with Goulbouddine Hekmatyar whose political party preaches the most radical Islamism. In 1990, he stayed in Sudan, where he became acquainted with Hassan Attourabi who welcomed him in his party, "The National Islamic Front." At the same time, he continued to supervise the weapons deliveries related to the opium traffic in the province of Helmand, which was under the protection of his friend Hekmatyar. (This reminds us of Hassan Sabbah) From 1990 to 1991, he often traveled in his private jet between London and Istanbul, where the American intelligence agents, Prince Turki and Osama bin Laden met secretly. The topic they discussed concerned the fate of the Arabian fighters in Afghanistan. Starting from 1992, he settled in Khartoum (Sudan) in order to intensify his fundamentalist activities in Somalia and from there, the rest of Black Africa. He also financed the armed Islamic group in Algeria. He did not stop financing "the Preaching Commissions" (*Lajnat al-Daaoua*) that regrouped several Pakistani Islamist factions. Since then, he has been nicknamed the "the Jihad's banker."

After having organized his attack against the Americans in Somalia in 1993, he was deprived of his Saudi nationality in a decree from the Saudi ministry of the interior on April 6th, 1994, pretending that "the irresponsible acts of bin Laden are against the interest of the Kingdom." The "interest of the kingdom" depended, in fact, on good relationships with the United States while bin Laden considered that their presence after the Gulf War spoiled the Land of Islam. In May 1996, he left Sudan under Saudi pressure. He stopped at Dubai and Islamabad before reaching Jalalebad in Afghanistan, headquarters of Hekmatyar, who was in an armed conflict against the Rabbani-Massaoud coalition. It is there that he gave an interview to CNN in which he declared "the holy war to the United States because they are unjust, criminal and oppressive."

This return to Afghanistan can also be explained by the progression of the Talibans that took control of Kabul on September 26th, 1996, to establish a regime that quickly proved to be insane but that was recognized by Saudi Arabia, the United Arab Emirates, and Pakistan. Meanwhile, the Talibans took control of the Afghan opium traffic. Bin Laden recovered this traffic through the intermediary of the Pakistani Intelligence Services because he was the "Jihad's banker."

How could so much money be used to finance Islamist groups? In fact, the Wahhabite Islamism, because banking interests in Islam (*riba*) are considered as a sin, has found a subterfuge for Islamic banks. When a bank loan is granted, the beneficiary has to pay for 10% of the amount as an Islamic tax (*zakat*) to a charity organization. These important sums of money are not mentioned in the bank's accounting books and thus can serve directly the financing of the armed groups in different regions.

It is wrong to believe that Saudi Arabia has really dissociated itself from bin Laden when the Saudi authorities deprived him of his nationality and when his siblings pretended to reject him because he was just their half-brother. This status of "half-brother" does not exist in a polygamous society where the children of all the wives are brothers and sisters. He confirmed this in an interview he gave to the CNN in 1997 and in which he revealed that he had received his mother, uncle, and brothers nine times.

The Saudi regime continued to support Osama bin Laden as it was mentioned by Jean-Charles Brisard and Guillaume Dasque in their book[19]: "In reality, the relationship with Osama bin Laden has always existed. As indicated by him in a note emanating from a western intelligence service, the bin

[19] Brisard, Jean-Charles et Dasque, Guillaume, *Bin Laden: la vérité interdite*, Denoël impacts, 2001

Laden family has rigorously applied, since the beginning of the 80s, the principle of total solidarity with the family members." As he is very powerful, very close to the Saudi rulers, he acted with the consent of the Saudi authority, exactly like the powerful Ben Mahfouz's family that happens to originate from Hadramaut. The latter supplies the Islamist Internationale with a great part of its funds from Khalid Ibn Mahfouz, the equivalent of Osama bin Laden, who was appointed as a member of Aramco's supreme council by King Fahd in 1989.

As for the features that Osama bin Laden shares with the other fanatic Islamists, we can keep in mind what has already been developed: a stagnation in the anal-sadistic stage whose adult paranoid functioning is centered on the phobia of women justified by the sexual difference which is seen as a shameful disgrace.

Because women are considered as sex objects, they have to hide all the parts of their bodies in order not to tempt men sexually. This is the only way to avoid a guilty feeling towards religion. It is the woman's duty to help the man control his emotions and his sexual urges. This reminds us of the original sin when Adam was diverted from God's Law by Eve. In fact, the Islamist men are very irritated by the sexual desire that women raise in them. This is at the origin of the rejection of otherness and of what is different. Because the fanatic person did grow up in a cultural environment that would help him overcome this frustration, he is unable to accept any ideas which go against the "truth" in which he believes. The woman is considered as a mother and then as a traitoress while educating her son. The betrayal occurs at least three times: first, after a very long nursing when she imposes on her son a brutal severance; second, after having been pampered in the women's clan, the small boy is excluded from it, and the boy then finds himself in the men's clan, which is a puritan world that considers the sexual difference as shameful. This is probably the origin of the frequent cases of homosexuality in the Arab Moslem world.

With this background it is easy to understand the status of women in Saudi Arabia and Afghanistan and to imagine a society of men anguished by their frustrations and yearning to prove their powers. As to circumcision, it is considered as the third treachery of the mother. Circumcision in Islam is performed on the child at a much later age to distinguish itself from Judaic circumcision. It is thus performed at an age when the young boy's maternal Oedipal investment is most intense. She is seen to participate in this bloody and painful bodily mutilation. Here it is useful to recall the original sin, for circumcision appears as a genuine castration, and even a corporeal punishment of desire. It is a young man made vulnerable, immature, and capricious, and in no way prepared for marriage that we find on the wedding night. Worse still, it is from this very individual that the community expects a rapid deflowering (is the brevity of the act assumed to be a sign of sexual power?) of a woman chosen authoritatively for him by his family.

Is it his own power or that of all men, I do not pretend to know. It is enough to say that a sexual act that is performed in pain and blood and contempt can only lead to a predictable hatred between the two sexes.

Here we are faced with a man who has not been encouraged to mature, and who on manifold occasions has felt betrayed by a strongly desired mother, without ever evacuating his aggressiveness towards her because of the cultural and religious taboos. The woman he wins, therefore, and all other women will be the recipient of this unleashed aggression; and as it is women who give life, the man becomes unconsciously a destroyer of life, that is, a terrorist. All this is sustained by original guilt blamed on Eve who was expelled from Eden for her curiosity, an expulsion that befell all of the human race and brought woe into the world. This is perhaps why fanatic martyrs (*shahid*) expect to be rewarded in paradise by having at their disposal 72 virgins and 72 wives. But what is the recompense for Moslem women?

This also explains the fanatic's denial of others and the suspicion towards them, especially when the latter express new or contrary opinions. Fanatics refuse all contradictory debate in their belief that they hold pure truth that admits no discussion. They claim a special status that their ancestors were forced to abandon – the loss of paradise and the loss of Anadalusia. These losses are reawakened now by the jeopardy of losing Jerusalem in the conflict between Israel and the Palestinians.

The personality structure of fanatics, in general, lacks suppleness; it is rigid with strong convictions based on false judgments. The fanatic's objective is merely to use others in order to gain entry to paradise by whatever means, including terrorism and murder. Fanatics are even capable of rejoicing when they inflict pain and harm on the other.

They are in fact delirious, strengthened by an unshaken conviction that develops in the coherence and clarity of their aims. Theirs is a delirium of requisition that skims over reality in order to transgress it. Thus fanatics appear as stiff, susceptible, vindictive, hateful, and idealistic individuals. This is what is called a paranoid personality which results from a fixation on the sadist anal retention phase that I have outlined earlier. It is a personality characterized by suspicion, excessive pride, psychic rigidity, and utter falsehood of judgment where delusions develop and take over the whole space of the persona after a failure.

They are often passionate idealists whose delusions may be assimilated to an imaginary ideal self. This delusion starts from an inferiority complex with all its anguish to grow by overcompensation into an aggressive and power hungry ego. Very often persecution themes symbolize a defense against homosexuality among personalities that share everything among males. They also very often present delusions systematized into sectors (in this case the demonization of the United States), sometimes having to do with real facts, which is some sort of logical conviction according to which all distressing sensations are attributed to a malevolent action.

As a matter of fact, these fanatics have been encouraged in their delusion by Islamist Wahhabite ideology, which has set up this aggressive machine in order to reach an ideological objective that Richard Labevière[20] has neatly summed up: an Islamism that is soluble in capitalism; an Islamism that is an antidote to nationalist temptations; finally, an Islamism that stands as a defense wall against the always possible return of socialism; in sum, an Islamism that would be the indispensable ally of neo-liberal renewal. One sees from this that the objective of this ideology is the continuation of the control and mastery of oil, whatever the race, religion, or culture of the victims. That is why it is useful to recall that the first victims were the Moslems of Afghanistan who were on the path of modernity, a modernity attested to by the fact that in the 1960s and 1970s Afghanistan was at the heart of many European leaders. The people of Afghanistan have since been subjected to communism and Soviet intervention, and then with Saudi and American money, the Talibans sent the country back to the Stone Age, killing all the men who did not share their ideology and raping women and little girls.

The same bin Laden with his Islamist nebula is at the origin of the killing of no fewer than 100,000 Moslems in Algeria. He is thus a political ideologue who cynically has completely disregarded the charia law which expressly forbids the killing of a Moslem by another Moslem.

[20] Labevière, Richard, *Les dollars de la terreur*, Grasset, 2001

As to the double discourse of the Al-Azhar ulemas, it reveals its duplicity when instead of making licit the elimination of bin Laden as murderer, they propose a consultation (*fatwa*) which forbids all Moslem countries to take part in a coalition against him, the very bin Laden who was never troubled when he had been the ally of the United States against Afghan people. In their intolerance, these ulemas have forgotten that it is the Americans (and not Europeans or Moslems) who saved the Moslems of Bosnia Herzegovina and Kosovo, going as far as apprehending Milosevic and bringing him to the International Penal Tribunal.

The same Al-Azhar ulemas are under the dominion of the financial power of Wahhabism, this obscurantist ideology that condemns homosexuals and emancipated women who aspire to a more dignified social status.

In my opinion, bin Laden has imitated his murderous ancestor when he abolished the charia law and declared what he called a reign of truth and last judgment. It is clear that the first victims of radical Islamism have been Moslems before it turned to Americans.

For this reason I am deeply convinced that there can be no such thing as a moderate Islamism, and that such an illusion is the fabrication of political "double-speak." To be convinced, one example suffices: let us consider the so-called moderate Tunisian Islamism.

I have been for a long time intrigued by the fact that those who were able to escape from Tunisia after persecution then ceased all activities that would harass the regime that had oppressed them and that has still kept a vast number of them in its prisons. We have the answer now ten years later: We discover them integrated by dozens in the network of international terrorists with far more triumphal objectives. Their terrorist goals are plain when we recall that Tourabi, of

Sudan, has been able to weave friendly links between the Tunisian Ghannouchi and the Saudi bin Laden.

In trying to draw a psychological profile of the enemy of the human race, I can only repeat what C. G. Jung[21] said about Hitler: "He is of the category of medicine man, of the mystic (I would say of the visionary), of the prophet. There is something dreamy in his eyes ... They mirror that inferiority complex that is such a strong characteristic in them ... He is the loud speaker that amplifies the inaudible murmuring of the German soul and renders them audible to the ear of the German unconscious ... Hitler's religion is the closest that can be to (radical) Islam, realistic, earthly, promising the maximum rewards in this life, but with this Moslem type of Valhalla that deserving Germans may have access to and continue to taste pleasures. Like Islam, his religion preaches the virtue of the sword."

The inferiority complex of the postcolonial subject is what may termed the complex of the younger brother who is always late to the feast, and who therefore tries to spoil it. Bin Laden experiments with and applies what the Islamists have theorized whatever their degree of extremism. This is another reason why there can be no moderate Islamism, certainly not Saudi Wahhabism which has been the main ideological and financial source (albeit in an underhanded way) of bin Laden. Osama bin Laden says and does in the open what they dare not say publicly or say only in "double-talk." He is their shadow.

It is ultimately this feeling of desired triumph (and associated guilt) that explain the solidarity among the Islamists who tirelessly exaggerate their predecessors' merits in an idealizing identification with their ancestors. It is true that the Tunisian security forces have been able to put an end to their dealings and avoid the worst, but they have not been able to

---

[21] Jung C. Gustav, *Jung parle, rencontres et interviews*, Buchet/Chastel, 1995

wholly eradicate the phenomenon, which, in my own opinion, can only be achieved through a democratic public debate that would once and for all expose the Islamists to careful scrutiny.

To understand finally the Moslem mind one must take account of two elements: the first is the opacity principle, according to which every Arab Moslem must prefer to abide by the injunction that if you sin, be discreet; this, of course, is a complete negation of ethics, for here everything is licit on condition that it is done with discretion. This principle is a profound hindrance to freedom of expression and serves to hide from view serious perversions, such as pedophilia and zoophilia (which may also be accounted for by sexual and emotional frustration). The second element is the Arab and Moslem persistent preference for the lunar calendar, which, by making reference to the night, stands as a death symbol, in contradistinction to the West, which has chosen the solar cycle. The cycle of the sun hero, according to Jung, stands as the myth of death and rebirth. But the Arabs and Moslems have a radical symbolic obsession with death. What is ironic is that astronomy was a thriving science when Islamic civilization was at its zenith, but it is now rather disregarded. Tunisian President Habib Bourguiba used to joke about the use of the lunar calendar, suggesting that since the feast of the Prophet's birthday occurs in different seasons, one must infer that the Prophet was born more than once.

Psychoanalysis of Arab Moslem Culture

The explicit demand of Moslems is to live in peace, even with Islamism and Islamist terrorism. Indeed, it is Moslems, as I have shown, who ultimately bear the brunt, in a sacrificial manner, of radical Islam.

The central issue, in my opinion, is situated at that level, that is at the level of the question of expiation and sacrifice. Islamists live and move around the need for sacrifice. They project their shadow onto the West, the scapegoat which is seen as their persecutor with its modernity which they fear or to which they cannot adapt. They react with violence and real sacrifice but they are in a genuine phase of regression. The only sacrifice they need is symbolic, a sacrifice that would eventually enable them to break away from the "Oumma" (in Arabic "mother," which also designates the Moslem community), which was able to reign as a great civilization from the seventh to the fourteenth century. Without this sacrifice, the Arab Moslem community remains as one single culture which is fixated at the anal-sadistic phase and which has lived regressively since the tenth century. For Freud, this regression would ultimately stop at the phase of fixation, whereas Jung goes further and deeper into the collective unconscious, as Susanne Kacirek[22] points out: "For Jung in 1912, even as he was moving away from Freud, still takes into account the labor of instincts during regression and of their double relation to the external object and to the archetypal imagination."

The Islamist lives for the objective of realizing an "egalitarian theocracy" founded on submission and obedience to God. He seeks to observe scrupulously the "charia" precepts (*Koran* and the tradition of the Prophet), and any deviation from them is considered as sacrilegious.

But literal and reactionary interpretations have kept every Moslem and all terra Islamic (*Dar Islam*) from seeking peace on earth and have instead led to war (*Dar El-Harb*). One only needs to take a look at Mawlana Mawdudi's discourse[23] to

---

[22] Kacirek, Susanne, "Origine de la théorie junguienne de la régression," in *Cahiers de psychologie jungienne* n° 47, 1985, pp. 29-45

[23] Maoudoudi, Maoulana; *Comprendre l'Islam*, édité par une fondation islamique siégeant à Leicester (UK). En France traduit et distribué sous le manteau entre islamistes

understand this: "If you have grasped the very nature of a Moslem, you would be convinced that he cannot live in humiliation, bondage or submission; he is destined to become the master, and no earthly power will be able to dominate or subjugate him." Such assertions sustain the unflinching and powerful determination of radical Islamists. Islam therefore has developed an archaic response to its difficulties of adaptation, integration, and progress in the modern world. It has retained a sacrificial character in the way it has singled out different scapegoats regarded as the cause of its grief, scapegoats on whom to unleash its violence. In René Girard's words[24]: "Religion is the means invented by men to extirpate themselves from mimetic violence and regulate human denial." The Islamic world has not found the time nor the intellectual instrumentality to rethink the illusory effects of its sacrificial mechanisms, which, in my opinion, go back to pre-Islamic reflexes in Arabia where space was empty and violence regulated social relations among tribes. Now Islam must be able to control its foundational violence in order to have a chance to return to the fold of history, just as a human being must control his or her own emotions in order to communicate with another human being.

The error would be in fact to respond in the same mode, that is, to accept the pitfall of the escalation of mimetic violence. It is at this level that the West should play the role of the psychoanalyst who is not expected to interfere with the acting out of the analysis – that is the Islamic world in full regression. A regression is a release of energy backward. The energy I am talking of is libidinal or vital energy, and the backward movement I mentioned is, as the Latin etymology of the word "regression" indicates, a retrograde motion of libidinal investment. It is a motion that, according to Jung, awakens archaic psychic material and makes it available for con-

[24] Girard, René, *La violence et le sacré*, Grasset, Paris, 1972

scious use. This regression, however, blocks the Moslem world in its forward movement toward adaptation, differentiation, and integration within the world community.

The regression I have thus far been talking about in connection with the psychological profile of the Islamist is based on the Freudian conception of a libidinal movement to phases prior to the development of the mature personality. When there is a regression to the anal-sadistic phase, we can expect the Islamist to project onto the West all of its problematic paranoia. This paranoia is due, according to Freud, to external frustrations that prevent all libidinal satisfaction, compelling an obsessive preoccupation with control. This regressive return would be an attractive dynamic movement toward a desire for integration in the material sense that Freud defines as the death wish.

For Jung, however, the Islamic world would have regressed to the libidinal level according to the same channels it has followed during its history, reactivating the nostalgia for unconscious material that belongs to the collective unconscious. Jung opposes regression to progression, which would be in his terms "a movement of life which proceeds in the direction of time ... and toward adaptation ... to the exigencies imposed by the conditions of the milieu"[25]; the Moslem world seems incapable of achieving this progressive movement forward.

On the contrary, the process of regression has been set in motion since the eleventh century when the Caliph El Hakam officially declared that "the gates of "ijtihad" (effort of interpretation) were shut." Three centuries at least were needed for the Moslem world's inhibited materials to become energetically overinvested, leading to an increase in its disorganization. The morbid and pathogenic symptoms appeared in the

---

[25] Jung, C. Gustav, *L'énergétique psychique*, Georg Editeur, Genève, 1993, références

fourteenth century, making of the Moslem world a sick man. Jung has said in this respect: "It is only when the individual (Moslem world) persists in that state, that one may talk about a retrograde development, of involution and even of degeneration."[26]

In its regression, the Moslem world has lost its vital energy which has returned to where it originally came from: "the primordial world of archetypal possibilities."[27] For Moslems this world is the first three centuries which are nostalgically valorized in the collective unconscious. Jung goes further in his work[28] when he warns: "If libido remains fixated on the marvelous objects of the internal world, then man has become a shadow ... he is like dead and seriously sick." It is this inferiority complex born by the shadow of the Arab Moslem world which finds an outlet through a compensatory mechanism and turns itself into the drive for the power one encounters in Islamist ideologues. Jung proposes a solution for the operation of the death wish when he asks for a symbolic sacrifice of nostalgia to liberate the vital energy and thus turn it into a progressive movement of integration into forward moving history. André Loupiac[29] may appropriately add: "It is such an imaginary position that the ego has to forfeit: he has to die to that very position in order for something else in his being to be born."

The Arab Moslem world must accept the sacrifice of this myth of a past power and choose between life and death, that is between nonexistence and a new life. For it is at the level of our psyche and our collective unconscious that this desire

[26] Jung, C. Gustav, *L'énergétique psychique*, Georg Editeur, Genève, 1993, références
[27] Jung, C. Gustav, *L'énergétique psychique*, Georg Editeur, Genève, 1993, références
[28] Jung, C. Gustav, *Métamorphoses de l'âme et ses symbols*, George Editeur, Genève, 1989, pp. 487, 546, 548 et 689
[29] Loupiac, André, "Castration et individuation," in *Cahiers de psychologie jungienne* n° 10, 1976, "Sacrifice et castration," pp. 43-55

would ensure our self-regulation and must arise. Jung again: "The instinct of sacrifice has at its source the unconscious."[30]

We must therefore relinquish the sacrificial drive that has been turned outward according to a projective and reactive model. The Arab Moslem world imagines aggression inflicted by the external world as castration. And we must replace castration and fear by a symbolic sacrifice of our nostalgia in order to liberate our energy and therefore our access to a metamorphosis of thought and behavior in the Arab Moslem world. What is required of the Moslem is not only to libidinally relinquish the mother, but to let go of the (archetypal) Great Mother too, who is, according to Viviane Thibaudier "the symbol of the source and beginning of all things, that is, of the unconscious matrix," represented in this case by the Islamic "Oumma."[31] The Arab Moslem world, I hope, can renounce the drive for power and omnipotence, for as Marine Sandor Buthaud claims: "Solution springs up from there and in an unexpected way. It consists in the comprehending of a central medium, but mainly the transformation of a position in and by the relationship to that central medium. In this sense it is a re-birth."

The Moslem male must first of all deal with the central issue of the status of women, for his regression does not stop at the mother but goes beyond this figure to reach the "eternal feminine." Conflict with the feminine urgently needs to be resolved, and Moslem men can begin by ceasing to project onto women the evil they harbor, the evil that is their own shadow. He may therefore access the sublimation that is necessary for all modification, for "the substitution of loving for the desire to be loved liberates the dependency on the other, breaks the ego's narcissistic closure of reciprocity and

[30] Jung, C. Gustav, *Métamorphoses de l'âme et ses symbols*, George Editeur, Genève, 1989, pp. 487, 546, 548 et 689

[31] Thibaudier, Viviane, "La notion de grand mère dans l'optique jungienne," in *Cahiers jungiens de psychanalyse* n° 57, 1988, pp. 1-16

opens up the possibility of emotional investment in the other."[32] This is also why it is vital for the Moslem to set up a coherent relation between his ego and the Self, between the unconscious and the conscious ego. It is the libido attached to the mother and even to the "eternal feminine" that must be liberated in order to enable the Arab Moslem world to let go of its hatred of itself, of women, and of "the other" in general.

It is the mode of regression that brings the Moslem to transgression, a transgression that he should redirect if he wishes to come to an awareness of his difficulties, to gain control over his impulses and to adapt and move forward. To this end the modern West must play the part of the analyst whose ethic is to accompany the analysand in his regression and to allow the latter to live again anterior psychic material while remaining analytically neutral. And this must take place within the framework of a transference that should not happen in hatred of the analyst, a hatred that is the essential prop of our dictatorial regimes that prevent Moslems from speaking out. This in its turn should not preclude the possibility for the West to express its aggressive potential, for "the omnipotence of the analyst may bring about the desire of sacrifice on the part of the analysand. It acts as a spoiling element...," as mentioned by Moussa Nabati[33]. The latter point may be construed as justifying the U.S. intervention in Afghanistan, which I consider necessary to demonstrate the power of the West; this demonstration should not go any further than thwarting the Islamist and trans-governmental Al-Qaida group. This is fortified by the knowledge that he who speaks is bound to remain calm and his internal circulation of energy should become more fluid. A minimum of freedom of expression must therefore be allowed in the Arab Moslem world; this

---

[32] Donnet, Jean-Luc, "Processus culturel et sublimation," in *Revue française de psychanalyse*, Tome LXII, "La sublimation," 1998, pp. 1053-1067

[33] Nabati, Moussa, "L'agressivité de l'analyste," in *Cahiers de psychologie jungienne* n° 49, 1986, pp. 37- 48

freedom can only occur with democratization and the elimination of tyranny and dictatorship in the context of a world
ethics that takes account of specific cultural identities.

If one follows my analysis, one may conclude that rigidity
is due to the absence of the democratization of public life that
is then unable to allow the development of the respect for
individuality and difference. On the contrary, there is today in
the Arab Moslem world a complete absence of freedom of
speech, especially when it is about the demonization of America, Israel's ally and protector; this demonization perverts any
political analysis and sends us back to the status of those
oppressed and ill-managed nations that let themselves regress
nostalgically toward a radical Islam instead of opposing their
dictatorial and tyrannical regimes. This confusion is patent
when one realizes the irony of the situation in which bin
Laden, a former ally of the United States, is declared the
enemy to be destroyed, whereas the Soviet Union, only
recently chased away by Commander Massud's Northern
Alliance, is the purveyor of their weapons and war machines.

The situation will always remain unchanged so long as we
have only an islet of democracy in an ocean of authoritarianism and dictatorship that can only give birth to fanaticism.
Indeed "a gentle and reasonable person may become insane or
beastly. One is always inclined to attribute the fault to external
circumstances, but nothing comes to the fore if it were not
there to begin with."[34]

This situation results from the West's cooperation with
totalitarian and corrupt Arab and Moslem regimes, especially
that of Saudi Arabia which continues to extend financial aid
to obscurantism by encouraging the mutation of nationalist
movements into "integrist" ones always seeking new "dawns"
in conformity with nostalgic regression, ever ready to reaffirm
tradition in the face of modernity because the latter demands

[34] Jung, C. Gustav, *Psychologie et religion*, Buchet / Chastel, 1958

171

individual freedom and democratization. Clearly, a military solution in this case would not be enough.

As to world ethics, it is a new issue that has arisen in the wake of the numerous mutations that have recently occurred and to the dangers that threaten the entire globe. This is due to the fact that international relations have become more and more global thanks to new technologies and to a policy accepted by practically all global exchanges; global thinking also emerges in response to the scarcity of resources, their rapid depletion, rampant overpopulation, damages caused to the planet, wars between nations, ethnic groups, states, and finally to poverty that affects the majority of the planet's inhabitants.

There are three theses to discuss here: the first one is the universality of an ethical norm. The concept of universality must be understood here in an almost "chemical" sense as that which enables particularities to be revealed. But the particular must not solidify into rigid entities; it must be approached, explored, put to the test, and sustained (in the double sense of nourished and aided). Universality which gave rise to the modern theory of ethics is today contested by the particular-izing critique of modernity. At this juncture one must address two apparently contradictory issues: the universality of human particularities, on the one hand, and the fundamental unifying need of men, on the other. The question that is raised then is: Can we dispense with world ethics today? And, does human plurality, and the different cultural values it conveys, oppose the monism of a purely formal ethical norm?

The second thesis, more recent, is articulated around the notion of responsibility. First, there is the responsibility for ourselves, our bodies and souls, our fundamental needs, and our duties, in terms of concrete commitments as human beings to the society of men. Then, there is the responsibility for the other, the ethnically different, the immigrant, the excluded, those who enjoin us to rethink all the dangers that threaten human plurality. Finally, there is the responsibility for the planet, the dangers that it faces, and the damages it has already incurred.

The two preceding theses bear a relation to a third one that invokes the thorny question of the rapport between ethics and identity. In this respect the first question of ethics is: "What must I do?" The question must be complemented by another one: "Who are we to understand what we should be doing?" Answers here are as varied as there are identities. What I am trying to attempt here is to shift the debate spelled in terms of appearance vs. reality, pluralism vs. universalism, West vs. other cultures, toward a notion of *identity as tension* between needs, habits, values, and rights on the one hand, and obligations and duties, on the other.

This the surest way to prevent identity from becoming an obstacle to world ethics, in the sense that identity presents itself as a monad that is a genuine "world" full of potentialities. This obstacle may be avoided at least by two moves. First, by the recognition of plural identities of which multiculturalism within nations and between them is the most visible form. One may formulate the norm first with an admission that "the other" will be different from us and still worthy of our respect. The status of religion in the manifold forms it takes, the usage of science and technology, and the recent challenge posed to mankind by ethics (physical and moral integrity) may be viewed within the framework of the principle plural identities. Secondly, there is the duty toward humanity that may stated thus: Do not do unto others what you don't want done unto you. War and peace, tolerance and intolerance, world civilization and unique cultures are themes that must be crossed whenever the choice is posed between a disinterested "duty of interference" and a cynical "obligation of indifference." In my view it is because the United States has not taken account of these two elements in its foreign policy that the tragedy of September 11 took place, a tragedy that sent everyone looking for the origin of so much hatred. Indeed, the Gulf War, which was legitimate in so far as its objective was to protect the world's largest oil reserves, failed in so far as America did not keep its promise to establish a "new world order"; nor did it find a solution to the conflict between the Palestinians and Israel. America was so "interested" in the Gulf area that it prevented Europe from reconstructing Kuwait, and as soon as the war was over, it moved to Afghanistan.

The Afghan war was the consequence of the cynical "obligation of indifference" of the West toward Arab and Moslem democrats who have been calling attention to the threat of radical Islam. European countries and the United states have naively protected and harbored radical Islamists. I was one who cried out his indignation and pain during a discussion on the Holocaust held at the IAAP Cambridge Congress in August 2001: How could modernity give birth to the "unthinkable," to Nazism in Europe, the Nazism that Jung rightly compared to Islamism in 1936? I declared that it is incomprehensible that the West would continue today to be complacent with fascist Islamism. It is terrible to recognize how western countries have flirted with and even protected the tyrannically oppressive and corrupt regimes which have given birth to radical, inhuman fundamentalist Islam. What I fail to comprehend is why, in the face of the threat from fundamentalist Islam, the western nations have not formed a coalition as they did during the Second World War when socialist and free-world powers joined in opposing Hitler and Nazism.

Recent upheavals have reactivated the question of universality in a world at once unipolar and threatened by the risks of fragmentation.

At the start of this twenty-first century the growing uniformity of modes of living and thinking does not preclude persistent regional and individual differences. Different cultures are as much moved by a desire for rapprochement as they are by the logic of closure and exclusion.

This paradoxical movement, which operates vertically between cultures and horizontally within them, does not seem to champion a unique world vision, though western hegemony appears evident.

Since the Enlightenment, western thought has declared itself "ratio universalis." Yet this reason which aspires to be exclusive has never ceased encountering resistance on the part of populations and communities claiming cultural difference.

One may therefore ask: What is the West's claim to universality? Would this universality merely be tantamount to westernization? And is this westernization a process of inclusion or exclusion of differences? If the later is the case, how could one even think of an encounter between cultures?

One could carry on asking questions about universality while trying to situate it between an existing reality and a horizon of thought: Does universality shoot through all cultures from the inside or does it structure itself from the outside? Does it require a "return to the source" or acculturation? What one ultimately needs to know is whether universality is simply the globalization of a dominant and conquering culture because of its technological superiority or whether it is a constant openness to otherness, an ideal in itself?

These questions evoke the thinking about the common fund of human nature, and they call upon us to investigate possible universal paradigms capable of explaining the mode of functioning and the evolution of all cultures.

Moreover, these questions, and many more not asked here, hinge on three issues: tradition, modernity, and post-modernity. Thus one may ask today whether cultural traditions, as a sum of skills and habits of thought, continue to be a reference for knowledge, identity, and legitimacy, or whether they have become obsolete. Also, it is important to ascertain whether modernity is foreclosed or whether it is still an ongoing process. And is this eventual foreclosure against religion open to another form of religious experience and expression?

All these questions are essential to our theoretical and clinical approach and must in my view be considered from two perspectives: a vertical one that moves from human history and psychoanalysis to individual and collective memory, and a horizontal one that seeks complementarity between particular cultures and a universal one. The connection can only take place in the context of world ethics that respects specific cultural identities. For this reason, I cannot but embrace the five ethical principles that Samuel Huntington and seven other political scientists have stated in their letter:

"We affirm the existence of five fundamental principles that concern all peoples without distinction:

1. All human beings are born free and equal in right and in dignity (First Article of the Universal Declaration of Human Rights).

2. The fundamental subject of society is the human person.

3. The legitimate role of the government is the protection and preservation of the conditions for human fulfillment.

4. Human beings are naturally inclined to search for truth and the ultimate ends of life. The freedom of opinion and consciousness are inviolable rights of the human person.

5. To kill in the name of God is contrary to the belief in God."[35]

It is the most blatant betrayal of the universality of religious faith when the last ethical principle is not observed. The observance of these fundamental and irrefutable principles would lead to the secularization of the state and democratiza-

[35] La Presse de Tunisie; rubrique *Monde*, p. IV, 25-2-2002

tion of political practices in the Arab Moslem world. Arab Moslems would then abandon the collectivism and communitarianism that has till now gagged them, and they would give more importance to the individual, who remains the first referent of modernity. The solution has therefore to go through the moralization of the individual, as predicted by Jung: "In truth, only a change in the mentality of the individual being can bring about a renewal of the spirit of the nation."[36]

There is in the Arab Moslem world a kind of dilution of individual responsibility within the group whereby every singular action is perceived by the group as a transgression. This dilution is due to the type of education which I have described earlier as a sociological education that aims at imposing a transmission of cultural heritage by authoritarian means.

As a matter of fact, the collective communitarian element remains very powerful in our society, stifling the individual who abandons personal responsibility under the grip of family intervention into his individual space. Here is an education that does not take into account the individual potentialities which are significant in our understanding of psychological education. The basis of the education we desire is freedom of conscious thought and expression, a freedom that seems essential for progress towards a modern mentality.

To avoid this resistance, communication must improve within the individual himself – that is, between his cultural heritage and his conscious aspirations, on the one hand and on the other, between the individual and the group wherein one aspires to autonomy even as one respects collective exigencies. This is in my view the only way to allow all the potentialities in a community to emerge. Moreover, by the prevention of this dilution of individual responsibility into the

---

[36] Jung, C. Gustav, *Aspects du drâme contemporain*, Georg Editeurs, Genève, 1990, p. 217

community, one surely avoids the mediocrity that becomes a general phenomenon of large groups and of the Arab Moslem world in particular. It is my hope that we may attain a better collective cohesion – more intense, respected and respectful, and guiltless – and at the same time bring about another mentality much more open to communication and therefore to universality.

Hechmi Dhaoui is a psychiatrist, psychoanalyst, and founder member of Orient Occident, a private scientific research group. He is an individual member of the IAAP, and he has written a number of books, including: *The Travels of Carl Gustav Jung in Africa* (Afanine, Tunis, 1998), *For a Maghrebin Psychoanalysis* (L'Harmattan, Paris, 2000) and *Love in Islam* (L'Harmattan, Paris, 2001).

Glossary

Arabism: The fixing on the ideology that calls for the Union of the Arab World in response to the feeling of persecution by the West

Islamism: Equivalent to the european word "integrism." It is the political use of Islam in a way that is revolutionary and goes beyond states

Maghreb: The region of northwest Africa comprising the coastlands and the Atlas Mountains of Morocco, Algeria, and Tunisia

Marabout: A Mohammedan saint; especially, one who claims to work cures supernaturally

Moslim: Normal practicing of Islam's precepts

(Moslim): Compendium of the sayings of the Prophet

Wahhabi or *Wahabi*: A member of a Muslim sect founded by Abdul Wahhab (1703-1792), known for its strict observance of the *Koran* and flourishing mainly in Arabia

Wahhabism: Fundamentalist Islam in the service of Saudi political power, to which it gives ideological frame in order to having manumission upon the Moslem World.

Ground Zero: A Reading

James Hillman

I

Two years ago at this time we were approaching the turn of centuries, of ages, and a panicky worry gripped the Western world. Not a visceral panic, one more sophisticated and abstract, named *Y2K*: Year Two Thousand. Would our electronic systems fail because they had not been programmed for these zero's in the date of the new century? Would this unpredicted zero make the data banks disappear and computers no longer carry messages? Would the system somewhere break down and instantly cause gaps and voids unpredictably elsewhere – bank accounts lost, electricity grids, hospitals, emergency services, shipping, railroads, government records, disease control laboratories, military defense, nuclear power, ... a civilization at risk.

One of my friends was a member of the White House committee focused on Y2K. This seriously thoughtful man was gravely concerned. One random glitch could throw the developed world into confusion, if not disaster.

January First 2000 came and went. The transitions from the nineteen hundreds passed without a misstep. No light went out. A triumph of rational planning and foresight, of technical know-how. The fears had been exaggerated, infused with religious apocalyptic forebodings. The world could proceed on its "metalled ways" (T.S. Eliot), and the demon Y2K had been defeated like an imaginary dragon, lying prostrate at the feet of heroic technical globalism. The stock market, led upward by faith in high-tech, soared.

Looking back two years, we should have snatched some defeat from the jaws of this victory. Or perhaps, the victory was a disguised defeat. The slaughter of Dragon Y2K blinded us to the reality of our fears of catastrophe, an enantiodromic, a world-shattering apocalyptic moment. For what did not happen on 1/1/2000 did happen on 9/11/01.

Profound changes in consciousness choose their dates arbitrarily. Historians who like dates claim that the 19th century began in 1798, and ended, not at New Year's Eve 1899, but when the Titanic went down in 1912, along with a great explosion in art, science and thought. 9/11/01 has become the date the eon changed. To come to some psychological understanding of this date, let us go to the place itself, to what is called Ground Zero, the physical center of the Zero Moment in the change of consciousness, the place of the Twin Towers, their burning and their fall. Once standing tall in the sunlight, gleaming glass and metal, brightly lit at night, overlooking the river, the harbor, the flatlands and the streets, such a tower was not the "orribile torre" whose door was nailed shut imprisoning Ugolino and his sons in Dante's *Inferno* [33:46]; rather they were extraordinary architectural splendors in and out of which each day thousands and thousands of people of sixty nationalities freely passed in commerce with the world at large. Precisely this, this towering magnificence of twentieth century world commerce has fallen, emblematic of falling civilizations.

T. S. Eliot uses the tower image in his "The Wasteland, (V)":

Ground Zero: A Reading

"Falling towers
Jerusalem Athens Alexandria
Vienna London
Unreal ..."

I must clarify here what I mean by a "psychological" understanding. Or, at least state what I do *not* mean by psychology: not a *psychologizing* of the *deus ex machina*, bin Laden, his motives, his family, his pathologies. Nor a parallel diagnosis of Bush, *pater et filius*, and mother Barbara. Nor do I intend to dissect the American character – its consumerism, its isolationist blindness and childlike devotion to innocence, and the irresponsible *laissez-faire* that accompanies that innocence. Nor its good-will Christianism, nor its optimistic belief in technological progress as solution to all ills, whether in marriages, hospitals or on the battlefield. Nor shall I rely on the Jungian notion of "shadow," that is, the mutual projection of evil and the mutual identification with God's will, as well as the globalization through sixty nations of both capitalists and terrorists.

These psychological accounts including the psychology of culture, Islam and the Christian West, fill the newspapers and are the property of elucidating experts, of which I am not one. Rather, I would explore with you the basic simple image of the falling towers from an archetypal or mythic perspective to discover, perhaps, what the deepest, ahistorical imagination of the collective psyche might reveal about what we read in the newspapers.

II

First the Fall, *la Chute* as Gilbert Durand discusses it in his masterly work *Les Structures anthropologiques de l'imaginaire*.

Durand, formerly at the University of Grenoble, follows the path opened by Bachelard, Corbin and Jung. A phenomenology of the Fall shows these motifs: first of all, fear, vertigo, loss of orientation. One does not know where to turn, how to pick up life again. There is an overwhelming heaviness, gravity and ruin, and the fall is marked by an inhibition: a refusal to ascend.

Second, Durand notes *la Chute* is a phenomenon of feminization, either brought about by female forces (such as Eve who supposedly caused Adam's Fall) or falling into feminine territory (Hercules, Bellerophon, and Icarus into the sea as maternal), or onto earth, *physis, material,* and into the body.

A third major set of themes of the Fall is punishment, so that after wild falling through the air – as for instance shown in Christian iconography – people land in the burning pits of hellfire – ripped body parts, pain, terror, ugly fumes, smoke and excrements.

We do not need to look far or fantasy much to witness the enactments of the archetypal imagination taking place at Ground Zero: panicked running, post-traumatic anxieties, the turn to therapy and religion to find orientation, dread of tall buildings, resistance to flying in planes, hunkering down in modest family relations, as well as the drop to bottom of financial markets away from high-tech and financials and toward manufacturers of common daily products. As for the feminization: it appeared immediately in the care and tenderness, and endurance, shown by helpers, mourners, nourishers. Restaurants laid out free meals, school-children gave their little sandwiches, vendors and suppliers opened their storage rooms and freezers. Strangers were invited in and given beds and clothes; the doors of New York, usually bolted, opened. New Yorkers paid no attention to money; value was returned to soul.

The feminization goes yet deeper, and perhaps needs to lose that gender description. Not feminine, but rather soul. The soul of the city emerged, the soul that inhabits the streets, the public servants, the common gritty language, the down-to-earth *gravitas* of Mayor Giuliani. Soul emerged from the ruin of the spirit, those exemplars of the top, the big shots, celebrities, executives, professionals, politicians. They seemed empty, posturing, vain – in some cases transformed and brought suddenly down to earth.

The third of Durand's themes, punition, also appeared immediately after the fall. Pompous preachers of the religious right interpreted the catastrophe as God's avenging justice upon America for its sins: abortion, faithlessness, religious diversity, gay marriage and homosexual love, promiscuity and adultery. America had wandered from its Biblical faith and was morally degenerate. On a secular level and without Biblical references, the left-leaning commentators also moralized: America got what was coming to it. It had been greedy and isolated, ignoring the plight of the rest of the world. From the secular and militaristic right came yet a different blame, again moralistic. America had grown soft and comfortable. It had lost its backbone, its muscle. We were too lax with immigrants, too focused on people of color. Our liberal laws handicapped the police and the FBI. The burning towers signified a wake-up call. This was a new Pearl Harbor organized by dark, strange and evil men – Taliban as Caliban – calling us to re-armament and tightened control of the population, its actions and its thought. Added to the pain inflicted by the wound at Ground Zero, Americans found many other ways to punish themselves further.

III

Let us return to Ground Zero and amplify further the archetypal image of the Tower. Some of the themes etched so clearly by Durand appear in the traditions of towers. For instance, the tower as anti-feminine, or at least inviolate, self-enclosed. Remember Danae, mother of Perseus locked in a tower; remember your Grimm Brothers' stories – the princess daughters imprisoned in towers by ruthless father-kings. The tower belongs to Santa Barbara, beheaded by her father. Barbara as patroness of architects is invoked as protectress against fire and sudden disaster. Did those who erected the World Trade Center neglect homage to protective powers, relying only on their genial design and construction?

Already in Egypt the hieroglyph of the tower is "the determinant sign denoting height or the act of rising above the common level in life and society." It is basically "symbolic of ascent," or spiritual pride, arrogance, hubris. [Cirlot]

Towers dominated many cities of Italy between 1160 and 1260 – including Milan. The Bologna tower of Asinella reached almost 100 meters. The Feudal period with its hierarchy of relationships, its aspiring theological and architectural structures was a time of tall towers. Later as part of the rebellion against the *consorterie* of ruling families, the height of towers was brought under civil rule. Many were lowered, their upper reaches decapitated or altogether torn down.

The towers alone do not tell the whole story of the falling. There is also fire, the immediate cause of the fall. Engineers say that had the planes not carried such a huge volume of incendiary fuel, the towers would have stood, and they did withstand the impact. But the steel of their bones melted. Fire brought them down. Again, T.S. Eliot's "Wasteland" – "To Carthage then I came / Burning burning burning burning / O Lord Thou pluckest me out. ..." Carthage – emblem of an eradicated civilization. How arbitrary the selection of those who were plucked out and escaped.

The earliest philosophical imaginers of fire were Empedocles and especially Heraclitus who asserted its pre-eminence among the elements. For him fire was a cosmic force everywhere, the soul or mind of the cosmos, an ever-living never-still kind of consciousness that runs through all things. Following this line of thinking, then the fire that brought down the towers has soul or mind or conscious intention beyond that of the pilots and the plotters, and an end in view, beyond sheer destruction, since in the pre-Socratic view of the elements, there is no fiery apocalypse as at the end of the Christian Testament, no *Götterdämmerung*, but an ever-renewing cyclic metamorphoses. The way down is the way up, says Heraclitus. Just as Pluto/Hades, God of the dead and the underworld is also God of fullness and riches. The Gods are not only diseases; they are also, after all, Gods. We are justified, archetypally, mythically, to expect something to come from the fall and the fire.

I mentioned Hades/Pluto, the God who ruled the souls in the Underworld. Astrologers keep an eye on Pluto as an archetypal force of terrible intensity. During the period August 2001 through May 2002, astrologers have calculated that Pluto would confront Saturn three times in direct opposition. This opposition occurs very rarely, and tension between these extremist planetary Gods is of the extremist sort. Saturn in airy Gemini – the Twins: the two towers, the two planes, the doubled insignia "AA"; Gemini, communications, commerce, neighbors, quick responses. Pluto in Sagittarius, far-reaching, idealistic, religious. The highest sign of fire. The shadowy underground figure of bin Laden with immense hidden wealth and disguised network takes on Plutonic characterization, much as the severe methodical generals and old guard of the American war machine – heavy weaponry, leaden language, long-distant, far-ranging surveillance – become missionaries of Saturn.

Order, immobility, structure like rigid steel opposed to chaos, invisible as anthrax, unpredictable like fire. The depths of Ground Zero smoldered for months and the terror still lurks in Plutonic tunnels. While Pluto affects the Saturnian Pentagon with "stealth" bombers, secret forces, and weapons that see in the dark, so Saturn affects the Plutonian terrorists with privation, cold mountains and barren ground; outcasts at the edge, enduring. Saturnian bones lie deep in the Plutonic depths of Ground Zero.

Is it not strange that the ground is named "zero"? – Zero, an Arabic gift to our Western languages and calculations. Zero from *zifr*, originally meant naught, a nothing, an emptiness without content. *Zifr* also became "cipher," the enigmatic sign that must be decoded. In physics a zero refers to a point from which measurements can proceed, either ascending or descending, neither positive or negative in itself. And the symbolic round circle in the Hindu mathematics from which the sign came represents beginning and end, both fullness *(purna)* and void *(sunya)* – number beyond number, essentially incalculable, of immeasurable possibility. That devastated earth in the depths of "lower" Manhattan is the zero Ground of Possibility, emptied of what was and filled with fantasies.

One final amplification, if you will allow: The sixteenth enigma or card of the Tarot, depicts a tower half-destroyed by lightning fire that strikes its top. Though the tower image is single, it is associated in occult literature with the two columns of Jachin and Boaz, representing the power of individualized life. Sometimes the Tarot images show pieces of the tower falling away and striking a king and an architect of the tower. The Tarot readings connect this allegory with Scorpio (the astrological home of Pluto) and supposedly allude to the dangerous consequences of overconfidence, or the sin of pride.

* * *

At the end now of these notes, I would like to reflect a moment about that extraordinary tower in the Bible, the Tower of Babel, and its destruction by Jahveh. You know the story very well, of course, but should the details have slipped your mind, let us read again the text in Genesis, chapter eleven. "The whole earth was of one language and one speech." [11.1] "Then the people said to one another, 'Let us build us a city, and a tower with its top in heaven, and let us make us a name; lest we be scattered abroad upon the face of the whole earth.' " [11.4]

The Lord saw this and said: "Behold, they are one people, and they all have one language; and this is what they begin to do, and now nothing will be withholden from them...." [11.6] The Bolognese Bible scholar Sforno (d. 1550) explains that this phrase, "nothing shall be withholden from them," means, "with such unity they can enthrone idolatry." We might pursue this curious relation between unity and idolatry later in our conversation....

Anyway ... the Lord punished the people by "confounding their language that they may not understand one another's speech; and scattered them abroad upon the face of all the earth." [11.8]

A short and simple tale, yet Babel has drawn many imaginative commentaries. For instance, the theme of the tower as anti-feminine: The builders were so intense upon their goal of reaching heaven by their own hands, that they would not let a woman in labor interrupt to give birth, and many women perished in the construction. And, the intent on which their minds were so set was to wage war with God and destroy. Evidently, Heaven is protected *not* by our climbing upward, not by striving spiritually, but by remaining in the polyglot world of diversity.

The image of a tower touching heaven appears in the myths of many peoples, in Mexico, Assam, Burma and along the Zambesi, for instances. Frazer collected these tales and reports on them in detail. The Bible, however, teaches a more complex lesson by means of this archetypal mythologem. First, the tale tells that the origin of the many different languages is God-given; second, that the diversity of peoples is also God-given; and third, as one commentary says, each people in each land has its own speech, tongue, *angelos* or message. Multicultural diversity spread through the world also results from the fall of the Tower of Babel.

At the simple level, the story seems to say diversity is a punishment, a curse inflicted on humankind for its hubris, preventing humankind from ever speaking with one voice. But looking more deeply, we can see that the Lord's punishment is actually a correction of *the error of unity*. When the people are all of one sort and have one language living in one place something happens: they become afflicted with ascensionism. They believe they can climb right up to heaven and take it for themselves. The idolatry of anthropocentrism; the disease of literalized monotheism. A people or a faith without differences, without division and dissension becomes self-assured and self-righteous. "Certitude breeds violence," said our great American jurist, Oliver Wendell Holmes. The people become *Himmelstürmer*.

To correct this vertical ascensionism that is the result of unity, the Lord scatters the people horizontally over the face of the earth. As in Manhattan when the towers fell, the streets were filled with a diversity of people from all walks of life. Helpers trucked in from far away – Iowa, Virginia, Canada. The city took to walking, the streets were filled. When the towers came down, spirit came down into soul. The city of

Wall Street plutocrats was deepening its values, uncovering another measure of riches in the Plutonic ruins.

God's destruction of the Tower of Babel is more than a punishment, more than a correction. It is also a solution. It offers an exceptionally valuable insight for understanding the fall of the towers in Manhattan. If, as Genesis 11 says, unity leads to hubris, then we must be wary of all attempts at unification – unified field theory in physics, single explanations of evolution in biochemistry and biotechnology, one true religion and one way to practice it, one interpretation of Holy Texts, one global economic system, one astrophysical explanation of the origins of the cosmos, one definition of democracy or of justice, and above all, one system of measurement by means of numbers for assessing value. "There are many ways to kneel and kiss the earth," said Rumi.

Each attempt at unity arises from ambition and results in inflation. The desire for unity expresses the latent hubris of rational anthropocentrism, attempting to conquer with the human mind the powers of the invisible world which the Bible calls "Heaven." Unlike the impulses of spirit, soul differentiates by clinging to matter. It spreads out like a vague mist in the valleys, the low and lowly places, wrapping itself into this tree, that look in the eyes, a keepsake, a photograph – a line of a poem – much as the people in New York after the fall wrote on walls, brought flowers to firehouses, put pictures of their missing in public places and mourned together with strangers from different nations and different tongues.

"There are many ways to kneel and kiss the earth." The earth to which civilization now kneels is that ground called Zero, the zero that in itself is nothing and cannot be fathomed and yet, like the soul, magnifies whatever it touches. Its hollow center images that void one feels at end and at beginning. "To make an end," says Eliot, "is to make a beginning/ The end is where we start from." [*Four Quartets* IV:5]

To find a way again after the catastrophe, let us stick with the image of Ground Zero. It symbolizes a wound in the deep tissue of the Western psyche. A wound is a break through the surface, below superficiality. It is an opening of heightened sensitivity, like an eye that looks and an ear that listens differently, less blithely, more acutely, and like a mouth that speaks the language of vulnerability. The wound at Ground Zero has opened into the depths below usual life.

In fact, so deep has the ground been opened that the Hudson River has to be shored up to prevent a gigantic wave of water flooding through the subway tunnels of Manhattan. In these deeps the underworld Gods reign. If we follow Jung's dictum – "the Gods have become diseases" – then the wound of Ground Zero has opened access to very specific archetypal forces: Pluto and Saturn.

How may we approach them so that our human world be taken less by surprise and terror? Difficult. Enigmatic. The ancient world considered Pluto invisible: he had no temples or altars above ground. Saturn was called Lord of Silence, a figure most remote. They do not appear, they do not speak; we cannot go to them directly. But they make themselves known as threatening presentiments behind daily life, as a continuing sense of insecurity. They are the ground of terror. Our vulnerability reflects their presence. So long as we admit the wound in the psyche we remain aware of the darker Gods. Unfortunately, vulnerability has been psychologized and labeled "insecurity," a symptom to be remedied. The basic vulnerability that maintains an opening to the Gods as felt presences in the world, this necessary vulnerability symbolized by Ground Zero, is being denied by measures of heightened security. But tightened security cannot keep out the Gods, nor remedy our susceptibility to them. Fear of them may be the beginning of wisdom as it has long been said, but it may also be the beginning of denial: planning genial structures over the wound and sending beams of light into the night-sky. Denial as pointing upward even while bodies are pulled from the wreckage and body parts sorted and counted at the carnage station.

"In a dark time, the eye begins to see," wrote Theodore Roethke in one of his most widely known poems. Ground Zero offers an image of the dark time and an eye that begins to see with fewer hopeful illusions, proud denials, and blithe self-centered ignorance. This place is as active and impressive as it ever was, its activity now in imagination and memory. It remembers both the splendor of the towers and their horrific fall, and the dead composted so thoroughly into its soil. The Zero encompasses all that fullness even in its hollow silence. It is a starting point, engendering both upward and downward. All we need do and likely the best we can do is to stay with the image, taking our cue from its emptiness, yet constant in our attention to the kind of vision occasioned by the darkness.

James Hillman is a Zurich-trained analyst and writer now residing in Connecticut. He was Director of Studies at the Jung Institute of Zurich and has been the publisher of Spring Publications since the 1970s. His numerous publications include: *The Soul's Code*; *The Dream of the Underworld* and *The Myth of Analysis*.

Religion's Role

in the Psychology of Terrorism

Ann Belford Ulanov

In the wake of the catastrophe of the terrorist attacks on New York City and the Pentagon, we can see how religion gets a bad name. Religious belief can inflate destructiveness to a cosmic dimension. Destroying innocent civilians gets conscripted into doing God's will.

Jung is noted for his deep, abiding interest in religion, both his subjective religious experiences which preoccupied him from an early age up until his death, and also in official religious traditions, west and east, conventional and esoteric. He sees himself producing "the facts which prove that the soul is *naturaliter religiosa*, i.e., possesses a religious function. I did not invent or interpret this function, it produces itself of its own accord...."[1] And Jung finds the facts of religion communicated through the psyche: "God has never spoken to [us] except in and through the psyche, and the psyche understands it.... [as] the eye beholds the sun."[2]

---

[1] Jung, C.G., *Collected Works* 12, *Psychology and Alchemy*, Pantheon, New York, 1953/1966, para 14

[2] Jung, C.G., *Letters* 1: 1906-1950, Princeton University Press, Princeton, N. J., 1973, 15 August 1932, p. 98

Jung sees us, then, as saddled with a religious instinct that can make us fall ill if we neglect, distort, or project it just as surely as will the repression, dissociation, or projection of any of the other instincts. Within our subjective experience, we must engage this religious instinct which is "a vital link with psychic processes independent of and beyond consciousness, in the dark hinterland of the psyche."[3] From an objective point of view, the side of religion, so to speak, we are also inevitably confronted with the religious impulse which is ruthless. It is born of Spirit which, like the wind, "blows where it wills; [we] hear the sound of it, but [we] do not know where it comes from or where it is going." (John 3:8) "Religious experience," says Jung, "strives for expression and can be expressed only 'symbolically' because it transcends understanding. It *must* be expressed one way or another, for therein is revealed its immanent vital force. It wants to step over ... into visible life, to take concrete shape."[4]

In the terrorist attacks, our social and symbolic space collapsed.We suffered violent disruption of our sense of boundaries, borders, and bodies, indeed of the continuity of our sense of self personally and nationally, and particularly poignantly in the case of our smallest citizens, our children, whose fate it now is to be born into an era marked by this shattering. To create a new social space in which symbols can grow, a space that does not take one opposite to the exclusion of the other (for people are praying to God from opposing sides), Jung says, "We must dig down to the primitive in us ... [to] a new experience of God."[5] Here we may embrace opposites and stand the tension of holding both in consciousness simultaneously until the new appears and we are both

[3] Jung, C.G., "The Psychology of the Child Archetype" *Collected Works* 9:1, *The Archetypes and the Collective Unconscious*, Pantheon, New York, 1940/1959, para 261

[4] Jung, C.G., *Letters* 1, 10 January 1929, p. 59

[5] Jung, C.G., *Letters* 1, 26 May 1923, p. 40

changed. We want a new emotional field where all sides are moved by charity to search out the truth, where all sides feel a self-restraint based on awareness that each of us can do harm.

To work for this space, we must draw on what we know about religion and its destructive side, and also what we know about psychic reality. We all face the question what to do with the bad. We know that none of our images of God can be equated with the infinitely free, unoriginated transcendent. What we do not know as clearly is that we also have unconscious images for God, both personal and group gods, our subjective images for the Holy. These images vary greatly among us and are fascinating, deeply personal and meaningful. They make the transcendent God near, alive, real to us.

What is extremely dangerous, I believe, and religious people are particularly exposed to this danger, is to forget (to be unconscious of) the gap that exists between our private and group gods and official names for God, objective images of God that we receive from our various religious traditions. For example, a child sees God as Horse, not a horse, not the horse, but Horse which is very different from traditional images of Yahweh in the Hebrew Bible as Refuge or Rock, or in the New Testament of Jesus as dinner party host, or God as woman looking for the lost coin. To fall into the gap between our subjective pictures of God and the objective God-images of religious tradition means psychologically we have equated the two. We have fallen into identification of our personal or group god with the God of official religious tradition. That unconsciousness will act itself out on our neighbor and result in theological bullying. If I have identified my personal God with the God of religious tradition, I will require you to identify with it too. If you do not, you are damned, infidel. I now speak for all of Islam; I speak for all of Christianity.

Subjective images for God can be anything – money, the market, Jungian theory, an addiction, a particular glimpse of the Holy. Such images are not the problem. They are the stuff of feeling related to the transcendent unfathomable God. The problem is falling into unconscious identification with those powerful pictures and unconsciously insisting we possess the truth that everyone else must identify with too.

Even more perilous is the gap that exists between all human images for God, whether subjective from ourselves or our groups, or official from our religious traditions, and the God who transcends them all. God is infinite freedom, unoriginated, immeasurable. When we fall into this gap, when this gap collapses, then our subjective picture of God, or our group God, becomes not only what we publicize as what should be everyone else's religion, but now our truth becomes *the* truth for all time. We not only speak for all of Islam, for all of Christianity, we now speak for God! We now possess God. I am now identified with the living God in whose name I kill myself and thousands of other people not related to my cause. Believe as I do or you are dead. Religion becomes a weapon, justified eternally. It lays upon us a duty to wipe out all who do not identify with this truth.

Here we see the destructive side of numinous experience. To touch the archetypal realm is fascinating and powerful and we are compelled to act it out one way or another. We can fall into a state of possession, especially if we are weak at the feeling level and also at the moral and symbolic levels. What we are unable to assimilate and channel productively falls into the collective, easily conscripted into becoming a power demon. Such amassed energy erupts. In contrast to Fordham's defense of the Self, terrorist attacks display attacks of the Self. Archaic energy bursts forth from primordial dimensions shattering collective and personal containers. One way to estimate the danger of any group falling under the heel of the power demon is to ask what place has the feminine been relegated to? How much difference is tolerated? Is there freedom to vote (which means by secret ballot)? Do the leaders leave the followers to be killed, or protect them and fight with them? And what is the value placed on this life here and now in contrast to all value being put off until a next life?

We know from depth psychology that the unconscious exists. It is a psychic fact. It is a force full of lively energy that must express itself somewhere. This force is collective in the sense that we all share in it and all our individual consciousness arises out of it. Psyche is like the body. We share it in common and we each have our individual experiences of it. Freud talks of the unconscious as body-based instinct. Jung uses the word archetypal to indicate patterns in which psychic energy assembles and displays itself, patterns which can be discerned in all the world's religions and mythologies. This objective energy flows through us, among us, and can roll us in its waves. We do not originate it, nor invent it. The unconscious is one very powerful medium for religious experience that galvanizes energy at a very deep level, at the primordial level that enlists our personal struggles and hopes as well as those of humanity.

The danger that looms when we lose sight of the gaps between religious imagery and the transcendent is that unconscious energy swooshes through us unchecked. Awareness of the gaps between our personal and group perspectives and humanity's as a whole, let alone the gap between our human perspective and the ultimate, affords what Freud calls the procrastinating function of thought. We cannot be certain we have discerned God's will; we need hesitation, meditation, consultation with others. But unchecked, this unconscious energy invades and inflates and overcomes our ego and our collective consciousness. It rushes through us; we are it and it is us, amassing forces like the full fuel tanks of a jet airliner, bringing down towers over a hundred stories high. The lives of individuals, whether pilots or passengers, are totally eclipsed. This force grips us. We exist in a state of omnipotent merger and we do not matter at all. In Jungian jargon, we could say the ego-Self axis has collapsed and no space exists for symbolic meanings to be found and created. Opposites collide and fall into a paranoid schizoid split manifested as the "Us-Them" mentality. We see in a TV interview Bin Laden gave that he was interpreting dreams of towers falling and of airplanes crashing as symbols of hope and power. At the same time people in this country were reported to be dreaming of towers collapsing and airplanes crashing, but the affect was fear, terror, "horrible vulnerability."[6]

Religion and the depths of the psyche act as resources for us in our present plight of grief. Both witness to a center of reality that exists, whatever names we give to it. Our job is to align with it and help channel its energy into personal and shared space to help with the lamentation, the mind-numbing grief and exhaustion, and with impulses to revenge and violence. We know from both religion and depth psychology the presence of this center. Both disciplines offer ways to affiliate with it to make a different social space than the one we have been thrust into by fear, destruction, and sorrow.

Jung emphasizes the crucial role of our tiny ego consciousness. We both know this center and simultaneously recognize our unknowing, for the center, the it, is beyond me, beyond us. Such a mixed knowing-unknowing means modesty in being sure we are not it. We are responsible to each other to prevent a psychic epidemic, to know about the center and that we are not it. For each of us immediate experience of that center confers on each of us a sense of the absolute, a mark of certitude. In Jung's terms, it binds us back, in the original meaning of *religio* to the dark and primitive roots of the

[6] Bulkeley, K., Paper given to American Academy of Religion, November 2001

psyche.[7] But we know we are projecting ourselves into what Ricoeur calls the "Wholly Other... to grasp hold of it and thus to fill the emptiness of [our] unawareness."[8] Thus we must bear the tension of a sense of certitude and unknowing simultaneously that breeds dependence on each other for we must contemplate and communicate together about this source we experience differently.

From a religious point of view, and in keeping with Jung's ideas for he says that "all religions are therapies for the sorrows and disorders of the soul,"[9] we must each name and identify for ourselves our subjective images for the transcendent, whatever we call it. For then the relationship with the infinite becomes personal, located, and though certain, it is relativized. Each of us will find her or his own peculiar and poignant picture for the sacred that includes our problems and our powerful potentials[10]. This is our contribution to the symbolic space created among us, resurrecting us into living vibrantly alive, both alone and together. For our God-images, both subjective and objective, make a bridge to transcendent reality and then we can house it, share it, dig it up, eat it, plant it, give it away, bury it as treasure in the field.

As long as our God-image lives in us unconsciously, it may stay with morphine or money and they do not take a personal interest in us. We do not feel known by them and hence we do not communicate this primordial energy into the world. "In the symbol," says Jung, "the *world itself* is speaking."[11]

---

[7] Jung, C.G., "The Psychology of the Child Archetype" *Collected Works* 9:1 *The Archetypes and the Collective Unconscious*, Pantheon, New York, 1940/1959, para 271

[8] Ricoeur, P., *Freud and Philosophy* trans. Dennis Savage, Yale University Press, New Haven, CT, 1970, p. 531

[9] Jung, C.G., "Commentary on The Secret of the Golden Flower" *Collected Works* 13 *Alchemical Studies*, Princeton University Press, Princeton, N.J., 1929/1967, para 71

[10] Ulanov, *Attacked By Poison Ivy, A Psychological Understanding*, Nicolas-Hays, York Beach, Maine, 2001, pp. 142-152

[11] Jung, C.G., "The Psychology of the Child Archetype", para 291

And if our connection to the transcendent has been shattered by the events of 9/11, Jung reminds us that just where we are "weakest and lowest; there intercession takes place."[12] Jung often quoted those lines of Hölderlin's, "Where danger is, there arises salvation also."[13] Religion aims at making the power of loving adult in the face of hatred within us and outside us; it aims at faith that the abyss of love is deeper than the abyss of death.

Ann Belford Ulanov is a Jungian Analyst in private practice; on the faculty and Supervising Analyst at the New York Institute for Analytical Psychology; Christiane Brooks Johnson Professor of Psychiatry and Religion, Union Theological Seminary, NYC. She is the author of *Finding Space: Winnicott, God, and Psychic Reality* (March 2001); *The Functioning Transcendent: A Study in Analytical Psychology*; *The Female Ancestors of Christ*; *The Healing Imagination: The Meeting of Psyche and Soul*; *Religion and the Spiritual in Carl Jung*, and other books.

[12] Jung, C.G., *Dream Analysis: Notes of a Seminar Given in 1929-30*, ed. William McGuire, Princeton University Press, Princeton, N. J., 1984, p. 506
[13] Jung, C.G., *Collected Works* 5, *Symbols of Transformation*, Princeton University Press, Princeton, N. J., 1952/1974, paras 630ff.

Stories About Stories

Donald Williams

Imagine a young adolescent at one of Pakistan's 7,000 "madrasahs," the religious schools that produced the Taliban and still prepare young men for military Jihad.[1] He wakes up with other children at 3 a.m. for study and prayer, breaks for play at 4:30 a.m., has breakfast at 7:30, studies the Qur'an till 11, sleeps for 2 hours, then prays, studies, eats, prays, studies, prays, eats dinner, then goes to the mosque to sleep. In the course of several years he will memorize the Qur'an in Arabic, a language he most likely does not understand.

Mohammed Ajmal Qadri, the director of one of these schools, a man who frequently preaches in U.S. mosques, explained that 13,000 "jihad fighters" had passed through his school. "Eventually," he said, "all people must become Muslim, including the Christians and Jews of the United States. ... It's our divine right to lead humanity."[2]

One of Qadri's students, 14-year-old Obeidulla Anwer, speaking in Urdu, explained that he will "fight for Islam and

---

[1] "With Pakistan's Schools in Tatters, Madrasahs Spawn Young Warriors" by Peter Fritsch. wsjclassrooomedition.com/tj_100201_madr.htm. The Wall Street Journal Classroom Edition, Oct. 2, 2001.

[2] "Pakistan's Jihad Hatcheries" by Ben Barber, a State Department correspondent for the Washington Times. www.worldandi.com/public/2001/December/jihad.html

for the pride of Islam. ... I will hurt those who are enemies of Islam. And I know that I could be hurt or killed."

Obeidulla was asked how he would recognize the enemies of Islam. "If I greet them with 'Salam Aleikum' and they won't say it back," he answered.[3]

It is frightening to think of tens of thousands of young Islamic militants who know only one story and will measure all others by that story. The terrorists of September 11 lived by the same story, could hear only this story.

I know, of course, that I have only to walk a few blocks to a nearby church to find worshipers also with one fervent religious story. Many fundamentalist Christians fully anticipate the End Time and the Rapture that will lift up all true believers and spare them from the Tribulation while all non-believers suffer. Fundamentalist Christians, however, rarely have intentions of killing non-believers on their way to the Rapture. They also know, like it or not, that other people live by other stories.

The more we know of the world, the more we see a multitude of stories. Each story, religious or scientific, economic or political, is an attempt to make sense of the world. But Qadri and Obeidulla, for all practical purposes, live in the Middle Ages (madrasah education dates back to 1200 A.D.). The "official story" for Obeidulla weaves the Qur'an together along with his needs for an identity, self-esteem, and hope and with the realities of poverty, illiteracy, and cultural isolation.

Especially as psychoanalysts, we may be able to appreciate the value and meaning of the Islamist story; it is natural for us to articulate meaningful stories about the stories people tell. An Islamist, however, is unlikely to enter an analyst's office because his story, held with such conviction, does not permit any alternate story. Psychotherapy of every shade is about telling new stories about old stories and about nurturing

[3] *Ibid.*

original, first time stories. The Islamist's story is as hostile to ours as our *stories about stories* are inevitably hostile to his.

Jungian psychology, despite modernist lapses, is at heart a postmodern story because Jung asserted our role in the ongoing creation of the world and because he embraced a multitude of stories – beginning with his theory of psychological types created to explain the differences between Freud, Adler, and himself and to explain the roots of their different theories, their stories. Consider the hallmarks of Jungian analysis: "holding the tension" of opposing stories and asserting in every session the irreducible value of individual experience. Every session of analysis affirms that each person has a story, their story is worth listening to and reflecting upon, and their story makes sense. Psychoanalysis of all persuasions is a story about stories.

It must be frightening to Obeidulla and to his companions and instructors in the madrasah to think that there is a global community of people who now move between stories as they might move between currencies and countries. Walter Truett Anderson has argued that the greatest threat to peace in the world is *not* the competition between religions or ideologies (stories) but rather the "competition between different stories about stories" – between absolutist and relativist convictions about the nature of human truth.[4] Writing presciently in 1990, Anderson said, "As we move into the twenty-first century, look for large numbers of people to be doing everything possible to turn back, as far back as the imagination will carry them."[5] The idea of the ongoing creation (or "social construction") of reality is, Anderson argued, "one of the most psychologically and politically threatening events in all of human history."[6]

---

[4] Anderson, Walter Truett. *Reality Isn't What It Used To Be.* p. 267.
[5] *Ibid.* p. 195.
[6] *Ibid.* pp. 26-27.

Obeidulla, the young Pakistani student, showed more psychological maturity during his interview than did the terrorists who led the attacks on September 11 – despite the fact that the terrorists were well-educated and exposed to different cultures.

> The boy was asked: "Since most Americans do not know Arabic and cannot know how to respond to the traditional Muslim greeting, are they enemies of Islam?" The boy looked confused. "I don't know," he said, looking expectantly at his hovering teachers, who also appeared confused by the question.[7]

When Obeidulla was confused by the question, he experienced a moment of self-doubt, the kind of doubt that the other terrorists must have habitually quelled during their years in the West. The young student elevated himself by answering, "No," when asked "whether all non-Muslims were anti-Muslim."

I do not have any trouble thinking about Obeidulla studying the Qur'an at four in the morning in the madrasah or preparing to serve in a jihad. It is easy to imagine him going to fight in Kashmir – for him it may be the only choice he has with his only friends. I find myself very interested, however, in how boys and young men survive a fundamentalist madrasah, in how they bear up under one unrelenting story, in the marks left by poverty, and I wonder how it is possible for them to imagine a desirable, credible future, if indeed it is.

What Can We Learn?

Unlike Obeidulla, Mohamed Atta, who flew the first plane into the World Trade Center, came from a well-educated

[7] Barber. wsjclassrooomedition.com/tj_100201_madr.htm

family in Cairo. His father was an attorney and he had two sisters, one a medical doctor and the other a professor of zoology. Atta studied architecture at the University of Cairo, graduated, went to work in Germany, enrolled in a technical university outside of Hamburg, and later graduated with a masters thesis on urban planning in an ancient Islamic city – he earned the highest grade possible.[8] This "gentle person," described by his father as "very shy, unassuming, and highly sensitive," chose to become a ringleader of the September 11 terrorists though he had many other identities or stories to choose from.[9]

Atta began attending the Al Quds mosque in Hamburg in 1996, immersed himself in a fundamentalist Islamic faith, and became a member of a terrorist cell. He visited the Al Qaeda training camps in Afghanistan between summer 1997 and the fall of 1998. During that time bin Laden declared Americans as legitimate targets in a "holy war" and the U.S. Embassies in East Africa were bombed.[10]

Unlike the madrasah students in Pakistan, who perhaps have had no choice but jihad, Mohamed Atta chose as an adult to wrap himself exclusively in a secret religious brotherhood of terrorists; he chose one story, one charismatic leader.

We can hear Mohamed Atta's wish for violent transcendence in the self-hypnotic incantations he prescribed for the other terrorists on their last night. Paraphrasing Atta's instructions:

Make an oath ...
Make sure you know all aspects of the plan well ...

[8] "Inside the Terror Network: Chronology of the Sept. 11 Terror Plot." PBS online, 2002, and wgbh/frontline. www.pbs.org/wgbh/pages/frontline/shows/network/personal/cron.html

[9] "Inside the Terror Network: Who Were They?" PBS online, 2002, and wgbh/frontline. www.pbs.org/wgbh/pages/frontline/shows/network/personal/whowere.html

[10] "Inside the Terror Network: Chronology of the Sept. 11 Terror Plot." PBS, 2002, www.pbs.org/wgbh/pages/frontline/shows/network/personal/cron.html

Read the traditional chapters on war from the Qur'an ...
Remember what God has promised the martyrs ...
Pray during the night ...
Remember God frequently ...
Purify your soul from all unclean things. ...
Remind yourself of the supplications ...
Bless your body with some verses of the Qur'an ...
Check your weapon ...
Always be remembering God. ...[11]

His instructions (found among his and other terrorists' possessions) prescribe the means the terrorists would use to dissociate themselves from the horror of their actions. Which one God were the terrorists always to be remembering? – certainly not the God of compassion we find in the Qur'an.

From scholars we will eventually learn more about Atta and the other September 11 terrorists, about the climates of family, religion, and politics that influenced values, beliefs, and private psychological needs. In the meantime we can reassess and extend our knowledge of fundamentalism in all its variants strains. Psychoanalysts created a rich vocabulary that helps us to understand terror, murderous rage, charismatic leaders, and submissive followers. We can rely on a century's worth of analytic thought and on such concepts as complexes, internal objects, persecuting objects, idealized others, false selves, projective identifications, the paranoid position, regression, the persona, dissociation, denial, masochism, sadism, etc.

We also have decades of research on authoritarian personalities, religious cults, charismatic leaders, small and large group processes, etc. Over 50 years ago M. Brewster Smith

[11] "Inside the Terror Network: Instructions for the Last Night." PBS online, 2002, and wgbh/frontline, www.pbs.org/wgbh/pages/frontline/shows/network/personal/instructions.html

summarized psychodynamic findings from *The Authoritarian Personality*:

> The authoritarian personality ... characterizes the basically weak and dependent individual who has sacrificed his capacity for genuine experience of self and others in order to maintain a precarious order and safety. ... Such a person, estranged from inner values, lacks self-awareness. ... His judgments are governed by a punitive conventional moralism. ... His relations with others depend on considerations of power ... in which people figure as means rather than as ends. ...[12]

C.G. Jung uttered one of the most precise statements about the nature of power in human relationships: "Where love stops, power begins, and violence, and terror."[13] This one line could well be the basis for new developments in the analysis of power in contemporary culture, contemporary relationships.

We can recognize the predominance of power motives whenever we see one person defining another. None of us are strangers to the forms of manipulation, deceit, persuasion, and intimidation that subtly undermine self-confidence and self-esteem. Our analytic training should include careful study of the moments and places where love and relationship stop and power begins. The psychoanalytic question to remember when examining the ways of power is: "Who is trying to get whom to believe what?" Whenever power motives prevail, then our conversations are exercises in persuasion and credulity, whether they occur in analytic sessions, across the dinner table, or on the televised news.

---

[12] M. Brewster Smith's Foreword to *Enemies of Freedom: Understanding Right-Wing Authoritarianism* by Bob Altemeyer. Jossey-Bass Publishers, San Francisco, 1988.

[13] "The Undiscovered Self" *in The Undiscovered Self with Symbols and the Interpretation of Dreams*. Princeton University Press, 1990, p. 57.

Our day-to-day conversations oscillate between power and relationship, between claiming or conceding power and the open exploring and revealing characteristic of relationship. As psychoanalysts, we need to bring skillful discrimination to all conversations and to see them as vehicles for defining what is real. Talk, we must remember, is powerful. Through conversations – whether "complex" internal dialogues or face to face exchanges – we constantly arbitrate the very nature of reality.

Wise as Serpents

Before his arrest, the failed terrorist, Zacarias Moussaoui, attended flight school in Norman, Oklahoma. Despite 57 hours of flying time in a Cessna 152, he was unable to fly solo – a task usually achieved after 20 hours. When he later enrolled at a Pan Am flight school in Eagan, Minnesota, with a desire to fly a 747, Moussaoui told his flight instructor that he was from France. The instructor tried to speak French with him but Moussaoui did not seem to understand. Moussaoui explained that he had not lived long in France and was from the Middle East. The instructor found it odd that Moussaoui said he was from the Middle East, rather than identifying a country. When his instructor inquired further, Moussaoui became belligerent. Later the instructor "tried to tell him he was wasting his money" because he was so uncoordinated at the controls and had so "little ability to follow the lessons."[14]

Here is where the story gets most interesting. Moussaoui's (still unidentified) instructor raised his suspicions with colleagues, one of whom offered the number of an FBI friend. When the instructor phoned, the FBI agent strongly encour-

[14] "Eagan flight trainer wouldn't let unease about Moussaoui rest" by Greg Gordon. Minneapolis-St.Paul Star Tribune. Published Dec 21, 2001. www.startribune.com/stories/1576/913687.html

aged him to make a thorough report but gave him the wrong agent to call. The instructor made three more phone calls before reaching the right agent on August 15.

"Do you realize how serious this is?" the instructor asked an FBI agent. "This man wants training on a 747. A 747 fully loaded with fuel could be used as a weapon!"[15]

Moussaoui was arrested the next day and held on an immigration violation.

How many of us would have gotten to the first phone call? It is exceptional that the flight instructor took his intuition seriously enough to go on thinking about it – the internal dialogue – and then to act on it. He had to go against the common tendency to minimize intuitions that will cause conflict, will require action, and will make demands on others. The moment when the first phone call was made deserves emphasis. We do not need to act on all of our intuitions, but as this story makes clear, each intuition is worth thinking about.

The flight instructor obviously told his story effectively enough to be *heard* by the Minneapolis FBI agents. They tried to get a warrant from the FBI lawyers in Washington to search Moussaoui's possessions but they were turned down despite continued requests.

When FBI agents in Minneapolis finally obtained a warrant after the Sept. 11 attacks, they found voluminous information on crop-dusting planes on Moussaoui's computer hard drive, similar to material gathered by the hijackers' ringleader, Mohamed Atta....[16] Not only do we need to respect our dark intuitions enough to explore them further, I think we also need, on occasion, to stretch our capacity for thinking about evil, for "serpent thoughts."

[15] *Ibid*.
[16] *Ibid*.

"Behold, I send you forth as sheep in the midst of wolves: be ye therefore wise as serpents, and harmless as doves." (Matthew 10:16)

Understanding the conditions for imagining evil may be as or more important than the task of understanding terrorist psychology. We have the psychological tools to understand Mohamed Atta, Zacarias Moussaoui, and Osama bin Laden but we lack trained means for an imagination of evil.[17]

It is not easy to be wise as a serpent. Few people have the imagination for evil that terrorists possess. Terrorists have this advantage over us: they have no impediments of conscience to violent goals – they can think anything. They have failed to learn to value themselves and others – the narcissistic dilemma. They have succeeded in learning to project everything bad in themselves onto others and to isolate their enemies within a fantasy of evil. Without the inhibitions of conscience, empathy, or pleasure in others, terrorists can think and act upon the darkest thoughts that the rest of us resist.

Fortunately, we can think evil and also resist it. When, for example, we felt the threat of nuclear war and studied its horrors, conscience slowed the progress of military strategies. For decades the U.S. and the Soviet Union imagined nuclear scenarios with great scientific precision but they also conducted "arms talks," signed treaties, and have avoided the use of nuclear weapons for over 55 years. As other nations acquired nuclear weapons, they too exercised restraint.

---

[17] Paul Oppenheimer (1996) remarks that the word 'evil' is reappearing in the journals, because of the "growing awareness that it is the only word capable of bringing certain awesome events into our sphere of intellectual proxy, of diagnosis...." he feels that "other familiar terms, such as 'criminal' and 'sociopathic' fail adequately to describe the monstrous acts to which they are addressing themselves." Appearing in "Evil as Love and as Liberation" by Ruth Stein, Ph.D. Paper presented to the "Terror and Aftermath: Perspectives on the WTC Tragedy" program, October 29, 2001 at NYU Medical Center. Published online at: psychematters.com/papers/stein.htm

Terrorists do not have the resources of nations for nuclear war but they may possess "dirty bombs" and a host of other weapons and credible strategies for mass violence. In today's world we urgently need to become more skillful at holding the tension between uninhibited guile (the serpent) and deliberate care for peace (the dove). Most of us are psychoanalysts, in part, because we come more naturally to empathy than power. From the vantage point of the post-September 11 world, I think we are compelled to extend our insights and psychological practices (listening, containing, thinking symbolically, etc.) to the analysis of collective power, of violence, and of culture. How are we to feel and think inside the evil we abhor and fear and still hold the tension? What is required of us if we are to anticipate violence? Can our thinking keep pace with terrorists who do not share our inhibitions, much less our values? And aren't we ultimately more interested in how the detective's mind works than the criminal's?

Projections

During a recent trip to China with friends, I passed through Langzhou, an industrial city south of Beijing with a large Muslim population. With the help of half a dozen people we finally found an Air China office where we could buy a ticket to Xian. The two young women who helped us were bright, animated, open, and generous, and both were Muslim. One member of our small group spoke Chinese, and as our conversation became more enjoyable one woman ventured to ask why Americans hated Muslims. She really wanted to know. And she wanted to know why we hated black people because, as she said, she had heard about what happened to Rodney

King. I do not know if she realized that Americans have been asking why Muslims hate Americans.[18]

In that moment in a small office near the bus station in Langzhou five of us were given the opportunity to meet and to dissolve projections in the warmth of interest and respect. I have no doubt that we were successful.

Generations of analysts and patients have concentrated on "withdrawing projections" and taking responsibility for the darkness we would otherwise deny in ourselves and condemn in others.[19] It serves us well to identify the "hook" for our shadow projections onto the other and then to concentrate the bulk of our attention on integrating the painful self-knowledge we gain. In the wake of September 11, therefore, we follow a time-honored liberal therapeutic impulse if we question our own collective violence.

But let's consider the shadow of our practice of withdrawing projections. After 100 years of psychoanalysis, we look for the weakness in ourselves so automatically that this "good" impulse can be used to avoid knowing what we know about the other. The "hook" for our projections is usually not a minor appendage but rather an integral part of the other. Our assessments of the other's shadow are often on the mark. It is, therefore, time for us to watch carefully the tension between

---

[18] See: "Impossible Histories: Why the many Islams cannot be simplified" by Edward W. Said. The article contains an invaluable critique of Bernard Lewis' writings on Muslim rage. *Harper's Magazine*. New York, July 2002. For background on Lewis, see "Coming to Grips with Jihad: Why so many Muslims deeply resent the West, and why their bitterness will not easily be mollified" by Bernard Lewis in *The AtlanticOnline*. Sept. 1990. www.theatlantic.com/issues/90sep/rage.htm

[19] C.G. Jung: "Nothing promotes understanding and *rapprochement* more than the mutual withdrawal of projections. ... Recognition of the shadow ... leads to the modesty we need in order to acknowledge imperfection. And it is just this conscious recognition and consideration that are needed whenever a human relationship is to be established." "The Undiscovered Self" in *The Undiscovered Self with Symbols* and *The Interpretation of Dreams*. Princeton University Press, 1990, pp. 56-57.

our shadow and the variable accuracy of our projections onto the other.

Analysts exhort patients to examine everything they wish to deny in themselves. But we handicap ourselves if we do not learn to apply the same scrutiny to the shadow of the other. We need to train ourselves to deconstruct our wishes to believe in the "good self" of the other and the other's wishes for us to believe in their beneficence; if successful, we may end with a reliable assessment of the other and of ourselves. Durable trust is built upon skillful timely distrust. There is a vast difference between believing in the goodness of the other and deluding ourselves by a *wish to believe* in their goodness.

We are trained as analysts to "hold the tension of opposites," of impossibly conflicting stories. Our daily practice from session to session consists in telling stories about stories. Psychoanalysis, therefore, is a postmodern discipline. Recalling that we are pre-modern if we live with only one story, we are modern if we live surrounded by many stories, and we are postmodern if we possess *stories about stories*.

Hope and Dread

"We hope vaguely, but dread precisely": I used to think that Paul Valéry's words captured the predicament of our time. I knew that our fears were astonishingly precise. Jonathan Shell showed us exactly what to fear in the 1980s when he wrote about nuclear war and demonstrated that the "unthinkable" was, in fact, very "thinkable." In *The Fate of the Earth* he described in precise, vivid detail the stages of destruction from a nuclear blast – beginning with the first second at "ground zero" and spreading out from the epicenter and forward in time through radioactive fallout and radiation sickness.[20] Since then we have become more acquainted with other well-defined fears: economic recession, overpopulation, global warming, melting polar icecaps, disruptive climate changes, deforestation, topsoil erosion, ozone depletion, poverty, famine, war, and ever more pollution of every kind. Our hopes, by contrast, have remained vague. We seem to have an impaired capacity to imagine a credible, desirable future, a future that would attract our best energies, our most sustained thought. I still think that Valéry's assessment is correct; however, since September 11, I think we remain shaken and unsure about what to fear and how to respond.

Integrating the shadow we project onto others is only half the story in any relationship. We cannot move intelligently in the world without also knowing the other and the other's shadow. We need to know at least as much about the other's capacity for evil as we know about our own. September 11 taught us that we cannot underestimate the violence in the world. As psychoanalysts, we are familiar with our extraordinary capacity to forget, deny, dissociate, and avoid. Perhaps we will not numb ourselves to the September 11 tragedy this year or next but our alertness to danger will not naturally remain awake indefinitely. In fact, haven't we already half-forgotten the anthrax contaminated letters of last fall? Perhaps we can extend our interpretations of denial and avoidance in analysis to include the terrors that overshadow our communal lives.

What else can we as analysts and as psychological citizens do to educate our hearts and minds for this new world? It is our practice to pay close attention and to reflect psychologically, symbolically. Although we most often reflect on intrapsychic dynamics or interpersonal relationships, we now need

---

[20] *The Fate of the Earth and The Abolition* by Jonathan Schell. Stanford University Press, 2000.

to think about the larger world we shape and that shapes us. The subjects of psychological reflection have to include terrorism, "isms" of all persuasions, religious traditions, historical tides, political movements, human rights, changing climates, and more.

The disenfranchised, threatened people of Afghanistan, Pakistan, the Middle East, and other nations and regions deserve our best efforts at psychological understanding – relationship, not power. Terrorists may make the most dramatic claims on our attention but our best should go to the people without a voice, not to the "martyrs." It remains our most important task to appreciate what despairing people need and why they need it and to give what we may spare when it is needed and not years later when they are famished and gone.[21]

Over time I hope we can find a psychological vocabulary and the practices to reflect usefully on the stories we tell ourselves and others about the larger world – a cultural psychology. Our analytical training always includes reflection on the unsanctioned personal stories that we avoid telling; we can now add the unsanctioned cultural and political stories to the personal stories we watch so skillfully.

When world events mobilize nations and armies, it is useful to recall that reflecting and interpreting are also mobilizing actions. We will do well to remember Jung's late words, "Insight that dawns slowly seems to me to have more lasting effects than a fitful idealism, which is unlikely to hold out for long."[22] A more expansive line from *Memories, Dreams, Reflections* makes a good companion: "We do not know how far the process of coming to consciousness can extend, or where it will lead."[23]

[21] *A Generous Man* by Reynolds Price. Atheneum, New York, 1966.
[22] *The Undiscovered Self*, p. 57.
[23] *Memories, Dreams, Reflections* by C.G. Jung. Recorded and edited by Aniela Jaffé, Vintage Books, New York, 1965, p. 340.

Finally, we can ask ourselves again what our consciousness is *for*. Our day-to-day tasks are often completed more efficiently when our actions are routine and unconscious. In contrast, consciousness serves us best when we face the unexpected, the new, and the future. As analysts, this is the consciousness we try to bring to every analytic session. We prepare ourselves to notice, feel, articulate, and contain anything at the edge of what is known, anything symbolically unfolding, present but not spoken, spoken but unnoticed, anything emergent. We need to know more about the mechanics of evil and the workings of power just as we need to feel the pulse of credible, hopeful visions of the future we may create. Balancing fear and hope, telling stories about stories – we engage in actions that are as revolutionary today as they were in 1900. We are, each of us in C.G. Jung's timely words, "second creators" of the world.[24]

Donald Williams is a Jungian Analyst in private practice in Boulder, Colorado. He is the editor of the C.G. Jung Page (www.cgjungpage.org) since 1995 and webmaster for the International Association for Analytical Psychology (www.iaap.org), and he has contributed articles to *Jung and Film*, *The Soul of Popular Culture*, *The San Francisco Library Journal*, and other publications.

[24] *Ibid*. p. 256.

Verena Kast

Sisyphus - The Old Stone, A New Way

Verena Kast refers to Sisyphus as the "myth of the forty-year-olds," who often experience their lot in life to be a Sisyphus task. Are our human efforts all in vain, or is there some meaning to be found? In the end, it is a struggle with death itself.

Dr. Kast interprets everyday events, fairy tales and psychotherapy issues in light of the Sisyphus theme, rendering it a kaleidoscope through which we can look deeply into ourselves.

Verena Kast deals with a problem that also fascinated Nietzsche and Freud. This book is packed with down-to-earth experience, clinical anecdotes, wit and insight.

- Murray Stein

120 pages, ISBN 3-85630-527-0

Alan McGlashan

The Savage and Beautiful Country

Alan McGlashan presents a sensitive view of the modern world and of time, of our memories and forgetfulness, joys and sorrows. He takes the reader on a safari into regions that are strange and yet familiar – into the savage and beautiful country of the mind. No "cures" are offered, but we are provoked to reflect on our roles and attitudes in the contemporary world jungle.

Alan McGlashan conveys a poetic vision which has more to do with life as it can be lived than all the experiments of the laboratory psychologist or the dialectic of the professional philosopher.

- The Times Literary Supplement

228 pages, ISBN 3-85630-517-3

Luigi Zoja

Drugs, Addiction and Initiation
The Modern Search for Ritual

Luigi Zoja argues that the pervasive abuse of drugs in our society can in large part be ascribed to a resurgence of the collective need for initiation and initiatory structures: a longing for something sacred underlies our culture's manic drive toward excessive consumption. In a society without ritual, the drug addict seeks not so much the thrill of a high as the satisfaction of an inner need for a *participation mystique* in the dominant religion of our times: consumerism. A far-reaching yet incisive cultural analysis, *The Modern Search for Ritual* is a vigorous exposé, drawing its methodology from history, literature and anthropology, as well as Analytical Psychology. From its critique of drug cures based on detoxification to its discussion of the esoteric-terrorist cult of the Assassins, Zoja's work is a classic in the field of psycho-anthropology.

144 pages, ISBN 3-85630-595-5

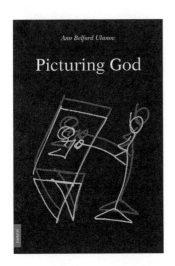

Ann Belford Ulanov

Picturing God

Picturing God demonstrates the importance of confronting our unconscious selves and allowing our images of God – both positive and negative – to surface. Such inner exploration reveals not only important insights about ourselves, but also pulls us beyond our private pictures of God toward a truer view of the living God. *Picturing God* shows us how to explore our unconscious selves and how this spiritual exercise can change the whole of our lives: how we respond to God, how we relate to others, and how we view ourselves.

200 pages, ISBN 3-85630-616-1

ENGLISH PUBLICATIONS BY **DAIMON**

ENGLISH PUBLICATIONS BY **DAIMON**

Laurens van der Post - *The Rock Rabbit and the Rainbow*

Jane Reid - *Jung, My Mother and I: The Analytic Diaries of Catharine Rush Cabot*

R.M. Rilke - *Duino Elegies*

Miguel Serrano - *C.G. Jung and Hermann Hesse*

Helene Shulman - *Living at the Edge of Chaos*

Dennis Slattery / Lionel Corbet (Eds.) - *Depth Psychology: Meditations on the Field*

Susan Tiberghien - *Looking for Gold*

Ann Ulanov - *Picturing God*
- *Receiving Woman*
- *The Female Ancestors of Christ*
- *The Wisdom of the Psyche*
- *The Wizards' Gate, Picturing Consciousness*

Ann & Barry Ulanov - *Cinderella and her Sisters: The Envied and the Envying*
- *Healing Imagination: Psyche and Soul*

Erlo van Waveren - *Pilgrimage to the Rebirth*

Harry Wilmer - *How Dreams Help*
- *Quest for Silence*

Luigi Zoja - *Drugs, Addiction and Initiation*

Jungian Congress Papers - *Jerusalem 1983: Symbolic and Clinical Approaches*
- *Berlin 1986: Archetype of Shadow in a Split World*
- *Paris 1989: Dynamics in Relationship*
- *Chicago 1992: The Transcendent Function*
- *Zürich 1995: Open Questions*
- *Florence 1998: Destruction and Creation*
- *Cambridge 2001*

Available from your bookstore or from our distributors:

In the United States:

Continuum
22883 Quicksilver Drive
Dulles, VA 20166
Phone: 800-561 7704
Fax: 703-661 1501

Chiron Publications
400 Linden Avenue
Wilmette, IL 60091
Phone: (847) 256-7551
Fax: (847) 256-1262

In Great Britain:

Airlift Book Company
8 The Arena
Enfield, Middlesex EN3 7NJ
Phone: (0181) 804 0400
Fax: (0181) 804 0044

Worldwide:

Daimon Verlag   Hauptstrasse 85   CH-8840 Einsiedeln   Switzerland
Phone: (41)(55) 412 2266   Fax: (41)(55) 412 2231
email: info@daimon.ch
Visit our website: www.daimon.ch
or write for our complete catalog!